INVISIBLE SOCIETY FABLES

PHIL CANALIN

DIVERTIR
PUBLISHING
Salem, NH

INVISIBLE SOCIETY FABLES

Phil Canalin

Cover design by Kenneth Tupper

Published by Divertir Publishing LLC
PO Box 232
North Salem, NH 03073
http://www.divertirpublishing.com/

ISBN-13: 978-1-938888-10-6
ISBN-10: 1-938888-10-3

Library of Congress Control Number: 2015931295

Printed in the United States of America

Dedications

To my parents, Anthony and Liberata: Thank you for always keeping a roof over our heads.

To Jessica and Kelsey: Your love and enthusiasm give me hope for the world's future.

To my wife, Sue: As always, it is You, forevermore.

Also by Phil Canalin

Slow Pitch Softball – More Than Just a Game (fiction/sports/humor)

Just Hug a Bubble! (children's)

Dinner at the Sonneman's (with Sue Canalin, cookbook)

Please visit Phil at his author website
http://www.philcanalin.com
and check out his blog link, book event photos and video, and
upcoming writing projects!

Contents

INTRODUCTIONS

Okay, shall we start with introductions? Let's go around the circle. Please tell us your name, why you're here, and anything else you'd like to share. Who wants to go first?"

As Marilyn expected, no one volunteered, but for some silly reason she liked the fact she still always tried. In her head she slowly counted down five seconds: five… four… three… two… one. Right.

"Okay, I'll start and then we'll move on to my right. That's you, Sascha."

Marilyn wasn't sure Sascha or any of them were even listening.

Sascha was sitting with her chair turned backwards, straddling the seat with legs split wide apart. Her hands were crossed and hanging limply over the chair back. Marilyn noticed her fingers and nails were black with grime, as if she had worked hard on a farm her entire life, laboring in dirt. In a way she had, but her farming was done on the city streets, mostly plowing for loose change and partially smoked cigarette butts along the curbs and in the gutters.

In the chair beside Sascha, Mrs. Kreiberg was using only her eyes to track an invisible gnat, flying in irregular circles just off the tip of her nose. Her mouth worked constantly, muttering low in a soft, rolling dialogue with nobody. A cheap plastic grocery store bag covered her hair, held in place by a red rubber band knotted at the back of her neck.

John feigned sleep as always. This was his usual defense system. His arms were crossed tightly against his chest, body slumped halfway down his chair. Dirty boots crossed in lazy elegance in front of him. Marilyn caught John's eyelids fluttering from time to time beneath the black baseball cap pulled down over his eyes, sneaking a peek at the group circled around him.

On the other hand, Marilyn thought Big Maceo really was asleep, his chair a miniaturized, playhouse version struggling to hold up his huge, bulky frame. His body was just about ready to fall off completely. If he fell, she guessed it would take more than all of them combined to pick him back up. And—whew!—Maceo reeked; he needed a shower.

Marilyn knew them all from past stays, except the last two: mother and daughter. Their sticky nametags read 'Lydia' and 'Rose'. She stifled the sadness at seeing them here at the shelter, immediately lamenting whatever mysterious past actions resulted in their need to stay the night. A mother and daughter. Times had changed, that's for sure.

She spoke.

"Well, most of you know me, I'm Marilyn. I'm one of the program managers here. My job is to interview you, get to know you, let you know the rules for staying here at City Search Ministry Shelter. I already know most of you, except you two, Lydia and Rose. You're new, so welcome, and I'm here to help you get settled in tonight. Next. Sascha."

Marilyn turned to the African-American woman to her right. She was wearing a black knit hat with the green and gold colors of Jamaica encircling it. The woman could have been anywhere from her early twenties to fifty years old. It would have been hard for anyone who didn't know her to tell from her worn clothes and even more worn out look. Sascha removed the hat before she spoke, exposing rows of tangled, course curls. Some mature show of respect?

"Yeah, I'm Sascha. What are we supposed to…? Oh, yeah. I'm here 'cause I would like a bed for the night, you know, get outta the cold. I've been here a couple times before." She replaced her knit hat, pulling it down tightly over her crazy hair.

"Great. Welcome, Sascha," Marilyn replied.

Mrs. Kreiberg was obviously off in her own world so Marilyn decided to skip her for the moment. Instead, she raised her voice a bit louder to wake the dozing John.

"Next, John!"

John slowly shifted his body in his chair until he was sitting up more but still keeping his arms folded across his chest. It must have been difficult to keep them like that with all of the bulky layers of ratty sweaters and coats he had on. John tilted his head up so he could see

2

everyone from beneath the bill of his cap. When he did so a swath of pink-tinged skin just below the neckline flashed, starkly set against the rest of his dirt-caked exposed skin.

"Name's John," he mumbled. "Need a place to sleep; cops been kicking me off my bench again."

"Welcome, John." Marilyn turned in her seat so she could face the big, sleeping body next to John. Again she raised her voice.

"Okay, Big Maceo, wake up; your turn."

The dark-skinned man was big all right. At least 6 foot, 5 inches, Mateo had a giant torso and ham hocks for forearms. No telling what his weight was—three hundred pounds, four hundred? His untied, greasy brown leather boots were caked in mud. Hands, filthy with long jagged finger nails, were massive, and he used one of them to push back the knit stocking cap he wore, a ball of gray cotton dangling off the tiptop. With the other hand the size of a skillet he vigorously rubbed the sleep out of his eyes and nose, and then daintily scraped the crust from the corners of his chapped and scarred lips. Maceo looked up and smiled at each of the people around the room in turn. Then he spoke, still slumped in his chair, as if it simply required way too much effort to move his body at all.

"Yeah, that's me, Big Maceo. I'm big and hungry and tired of sleeping out in the park. Jes' need a break, you know? Sure hope you got them hot biscuits tonight, Miss Marilyn."

"Yes, Maceo, we'll see what's cooking in a minute. We'll get you fed and a nice shower before bed, too." She smiled. In a world of heartache and struggle, it still came down to the simple things in life.

"BIG Maceo, Miss Marilyn, remember?" He reminded her. "I brought another pair of pants. You guys have any shirts or coats or something—these things I'm wearing are old?"

"We'll check, we'll check. Welcome back, it's been a while." Marilyn rotated again in her seat. "Ma'am, Lydia?"

The woman had a big, red down coat on, not in bad condition, and a pair of Eco hiking boots. She also wore a knit hat but removed it along with a matching dark blue scarf before smiling shyly.

"Hi, I'm Lydia." The older woman reached over and grasped the

3

younger girl's hand in hers. "This is my daughter, Rose. We haven't had a good meal in a couple of days and couldn't find a place to sleep tonight; thought we'd be safe here. I hope that's true. Is that enough?"

"Yes, Lydia, good," Marilyn answered. "We'll have a little more paperwork for you to fill out since it's your first time here, not much." She smiled once more at Lydia and Rose. "Rose, do want to say something?"

Rose shook her head. "No, not really. Just thanks for letting us stay here tonight."

She wore a gray hooded sweatshirt with a denim jacket buttoned over it, faded jeans and black boots; just another teenager on the street. Could just as easily have been returning from the library after doing her homework. Rose's shoulder-length blond hair was in a ponytail and covered loosely by a red, knitted scarf.

"You're welcome, Rose," Marilyn said. Then she clapped her hands lightly, three, four times. "Okay, Mrs. Kreiberg. Mrs. K, are you all right?"

Mrs. Kreiberg had gotten up from her seat and slowly walked around the small circle of chairs. She reached into the bulky black garbage bag draped over her shoulder and pulled out a handful of dark red rose petals. The woman then scattered a few about each chair as she passed, even tossed a few over John, who resumed sleeping.

"Okay, Ms. Kreiberg, that's enough. You know we're going to have to clean that up. Come on, let's get back to your seat."

Mrs. Kreiberg dropped the last of her petals at Marilyn's feet.

"No, no sitting. Got to keep moving," Mrs. Kreiberg told her. "Got to keep moving or can't keep up. World's moving too fast, gotta keep up." She continued her circular stroll.

Mrs. Kreiberg was an older woman, perhaps sixty, sixty-five maybe, wearing a long, ratty, black wool coat, every button buttoned from her shins up to her neck. She wore dark green ski gloves, each of the finger tips cut off, uneven threads hanging from the jagged edges. Upon her nose sat a pair of dirty glasses, with thick nylon string attached to the end of each arm keeping them around her neck. Her plastic head cover crackled as she shuffled around the people seated.

"Well, Mrs. Kreiberg—this is Mrs. Kreiberg everybody. Mrs. Kreiberg, you know you've been here before and have to follow the rules the same as everyone else, right?"

"Yes, yep, yes, we'll follow the rules. No problem, not a problem. Just need a bed, someplace to sleep for just a few minutes. Then gotta go. Moving on, moving out."

"Do you want to take a seat, Mrs. Kreiberg? Please sit down in your seat for a minute like everyone else."

"No problem, not a problem." But Mrs. Kreiberg didn't take her seat, just kept moving around the circle, now dragging her garbage bag of belongings behind her.

"Everyone, I'm going to have someone help Mrs. Kreiberg here. Just a minute, okay?" Marilyn got up, opened the door behind her and stuck her head out. She called down the hallway.

"Travis? You busy? Can I use you for a minute?" She turned back to the group. "Thanks, everyone, it'll just be a minute."

Footsteps sounded down the hallway and then a burly man entered the room, his hair long and unkempt. Two-day's worth of thick stubble grew on his chin and cheeks. Travis had on a big green Army coat that had seen better days. His blue jeans looked crisp and new, though, and his boots certainly looked like good Army surplus. A veteran maybe.

Marilyn smiled at him. "Thanks, Travis. Everyone, this is Travis, a new volunteer here at City Search. First night, so you all be kind."

Travis lowered his eyes shyly and gave the group a slight wave of his hand. Marilyn got up from her seat and took Mrs. Kreiberg gently by one of her gloved hands.

"Travis, Mrs. Kreiberg just needs a little attention. Her file and paperwork are on my desk. Can you see if you can get her settled, maybe find someone to get her cleaned up a little and ready for dinner? Thanks, I appreciate it. Give her the bed in Room 14, okay?"

"Okay, I can do that. No problem," Travis gruffly replied.

Marilyn tried to get Mrs. Kreiberg to look her in the eyes. "Mrs. Kreiberg, this is Travis. He's going to help you for now and then I will check in on you in just a little bit, okay?"

5

_ome on, Mrs. K., let's head on out with me." Without a moment's
.ation, Travis placed a gentle, deft hand on Mrs. Kreiberg's elbow
.d led her from the room.

"Okay, time to go, hair long, long hair, time to go. Gotta get settled,
but not for too long, get settled, get fed, short rest." Mrs. K continued
her pitter-patter out the door and down the hall until the group couldn't
hear her any longer.

Now Marilyn turned back to them. "Okay, great, we're all here
then. Good. You guys know the drill, of course, except maybe Lydia and
Rose. So when Travis gets back he'll have you, John and Maceo—"

"Big Maceo."

"Yes, right, John and—BIG Maceo—and Sascha, you'll need to
update your shelter cards first. Then off to the lavatories, whatever,
for 20-30 minutes."

"I don't think I need a shower," said Sascha. "I just want to wash
up a bit."

"Okay, that's fine, but you might change your mind later. Remember the water's good and hot. There's shampoo, everything. Anyway, after
that, then you meet back here for a little talk and video, just like before."

"Are we going to talk about crazy shit again?" Big Maceo's stomach
growled loud enough for them to hear. "That video was a waste of time."

"Not the same, you'll like this one. Besides, it's only 15 minutes long
so I think you'll survive. And please watch your language, you know
better. Following that, a short prayer service with Pastor Richard, and,
of course, dinner. Then in for the night, okay? Sound good?"

No response other than a couple of heads nodding. In that moment
Travis re-entered to the room.

"Hey, Mrs. Kreiberg's all set. So what can I do next?" he asked
Marilyn.

"Well, our intros are done here, so why don't you take the group
down to the lavatories. Shirley T. will take Sascha from you when you
get there, but you can take John and Big Maceo. Lydia and Rose." She
turned to them. "You stay with me to complete your intake forms and
liability papers. You have your TB test reports, I hope?"

The mother and daughter both nodded.

"Okay, then the rest of you can go with Travis. Lydia, Rose, you're with me. We'll all meet back here in about 30 minutes, right?"

"One question, Marilyn." This from Travis.

"Yes?"

"There are another twenty or so folk outside the doors, still in line, waiting."

"Yes?"

"Well, what do we do with them?"

"Unfortunately, we're out of bed spaces for tonight. Give them the sheet with the shelter number listings, if they'll take it. They can use the list of shelter phone numbers to call other shelters for available space."

"So send them away?"

"Yes, we only have so much room. We can't help them all tonight. We can't really help everybody that needs help any night. There are just too many."

Travis hesitated. "But these folks aren't going to shop around for shelters. And most of the shelters are booked up for the night anyway."

"Right," Marilyn answered. "Just like us. We're booked, too."

She had worked with many new volunteers before and always, always despised that exact moment when they realized they really could only do so much. That it was never enough. And they all had that moment, every single one of them. Somehow a few like herself, Marilyn supposed, immediately hardened and could hold that sadness and help-lessness in and continue to do whatever they could to help. Not many, though, from her experience. At times she considered what kind of person did that make her? Marilyn frequently caught herself staring in mirrors as she wondered about the true answer to that question.

"There are kids out there, too—young ones. Families, Marilyn." Travis' eyes pleaded.

"It's hard, Travis. I know it's hard," she replied. "But we do what we can. Let's get these guys going, okay?"

"What about some of the other space—rooms, offices, whatever?" Travis kept on her. "Any place out of the cold. A closet, whatever. If we turn them away they'll just find a bench or an alley, someplace unsafe."

7

"Travis, come on," she told him firmly. "We talked about this before you started. These people need our help. They came here, first come, first served."

"Well, crap," Travis said, defeated. "I don't like it."

"I don't like it, either, Travis. None of us do."

Travis turned from her.

"John, Sascha, Big Dude!" he called to them. "Let's go, you're coming with me!"

And as he led them from the room, he turned back one last time to Marilyn and said, "There's gotta be a better way."

"Well, when you find it you please let me know," she replied with a sigh as he left Marilyn alone with Lydia and her daughter to ponder their fortunes.

§ § §

Much later that night, Marilyn was working at her county office downtown, catching up on some work she needed to finish before the end of the week. She had gotten everybody in her group settled into the program at the shelter for the night before leaving. The other staff would look out for them.

And that included Travis, too. She decided she would talk with him in the morning, to help him get past what she knew he was feeling. To commiserate and empathize and let him know she and so many others struggled through the exact same thing. To help him, she hoped.

Her phone rang right at midnight.

It was Shirley T. Shirley T. was one of the Clinic's success stories, a recovering alcoholic, now two years sober, who had come back to volunteer as a part-time employee. Something was wrong at the shelter, not an emergency, nothing to fret about, Shirley T. said, but Marilyn had better come down if she could. She told Shirley T. she'd be right over.

Marilyn shut down her computer and closed up the office. She got in her small commuter sedan and drove the two miles to the City

Search Ministry Shelter. Shirley T. met her as she walked through the front door.

"Here, Marilyn." Shirley T. handed her a single sheet of notebook paper, folded twice over. "This is from Travis. You better read it."

Marilyn stopped to open the note. It was in pencil, in Travis's messy printing, and it read:

"Dear Marilyn,

I understand you all are trying to do the best you can with what little you have. I just know there's got to be a better way. I don't think this is the right fit for me, but I wish you and everyone the best. Thanks for letting me try. Keep trying, I know you will. And I will, too. See you in the trenches—Travis Waller".

Marilyn sighed. Too late.

"And you should come see this, too, Marilyn."

Marilyn followed Shirley T. down the hallway, turning left, away from the client sleeping facilities where it was dark and quiet. She was led into the administrative office area where the managers and volunteers had a few desks, did intakes and case management, filled out paperwork, and met with their clients in private when needed. Usually the doors were kept locked, because of the confidential information filed there and to safeguard the Shelter's office equipment.

But tonight each of the four small office doors stood open, low lights shining from within. Marilyn stuck her head into the first office.

When her eyes adjusted to the light and realized what she saw, Marilyn knew she had expected it all along.

People were sleeping body to body on the floor in the small office, wrapped in Shelter blankets and old sleeping bags, their heads resting on pillows and wadded up coats. Two others slept in a corner, propped up on the two chairs in the office. At least a dozen folks slept quietly, out of the cold night. She assumed every other office was the same.

"Travis?" she whispered to Shirley T.

"Yep," Shirley T answered. "Right after you left he went out and rounded up everyone we had turned away, and then found a few more. Got them cleaned up and fed them himself. Bedded them all down here."

"Okay for tonight," Marilyn wondered. "But what about tomorrow night?"

Shirley T.'s eyes sparkled with tears. "Travis said the only thing that mattered to these homeless people tonight, was tonight."

"Tonight," Marilyn whispered. And her eyes glistened, too.

ONE COAT

*Based on the fable "The Fox and the Grapes": The Fox realizes the vines
have climbed too high for him to reach the ripe, succulent grapes he craves.
So the Fox convinces himself that they were probably sour anyway and
doesn't really want them after all.*

The moral of the fable is: It is easy to despise what you cannot have.

D ang, Doc, you guys are busier than hell."
Sascha plopped herself down in the exam chair next to Dr.
Salim, already rolling up the right sleeve of her shirt. The
cuff was frayed and dirty like the wool shirt and the rest of the clothes
she wore. She tucked a stray piece of ripped material under the tight-
ening arm-roll to keep it in place. Her body odor smelled like her
clothes looked, a bit worse for wear. Luckily, the cool temperatures of
winter did much to diminish the odor.

"Did you complete all of the paperwork with Judy in the Intake
Room?" Dr. Salim asked, tearing open a packet of disinfectant swabs
that would be used to prep her forearm.

The doctor wore tight fitting latex gloves on both hands, tight
enough for Sascha to see through to her too short, non-manicured
nails. Obviously, Dr. Salim nervously chewed her fingernails. What
the hell would a rich doc have to be nervous about?

The Intake Room was the middle section of the mobile clinic,
cordoned off from the Examination Rooms on either side by now-
closed plastic accordion screens. The screens' half-inch thickness
wasn't enough to fully contain the sounds of the day's constant intake
interview process, handled by the social worker, Judy. Judy also drove
the van to and from scheduled sites.

"Yeah, we finished, after waiting for 45 minutes out in the cold.

Can't you guys get one of them electric heaters or something? It's colder than crap out there today. They got them heaters lining the front of St. Augustine's, so when you're waiting in line for breakfast, you don't freeze your ass off."

"It's always very busy when we do the TB testing," Dr. Salim sighed and pulled Sascha's right hand forward to stretch her arm out flat on the corner of the desk. "And we can do nothing about the cold, sorry. You're lucky enough to have the TB clinic out here every other week. Where is your jacket? Don't you have a coat?"

"Nah, Doc, I left my coat at the cleaners with my other furs and mink coats." She rolled her eyes and noticed the coat hanging on a hook on the wall in the back corner. "Now that there's a nice coat, looks pretty warm. That yours, Doc?"

Without looking up, Dr. Salim answered. "Yes, yes. Now, this is to clean and disinfect your arm for the test."

In a small circular motion she wiped the front of Sascha's arm clean, and then dropped the used swab into a small red plastic container.

"What size are you, Doc? About a medium, medium/large? What's that size, eight, ten? I dig me that little white fur around the hood, too. I bet you can cinch that real tight around your face—that would keep you good and warm. Good and warm no matter how cold it gets out there."

Dr. Salim readied the PPD injection. "Okay, this is going to sting just a little bit… okay, that's it. Over." The used syringe also went into the red container.

Sascha grabbed Dr. Salim's wrist gently with her left hand. "No, seriously, Doc, what—large?"

"What? Large? Oh, yes, whatever, yes, it's a size large." Dr. Salim lifted Sascha's hand from her wrist. "Now, if this starts to hurt or burn or get itchy or get really red and bumpy, please call back here or go to the closest clinic to where you live."

"Doc, I'm homeless, remember? No phone, no place to live?"

"Oh, right, right. So go to the nearest clinic wherever you are and have them look at your arm. But only if it is bad."

"Okay, simple enough. So you think I can get me one of them free coats like that at the office over there, doc?"

"Now you can come back on Thursday, after 1:00 pm, right? If you don't come back on that day to have the test read then today will all be a waste of time and you'll have to do it all over again."

"Yeah, I know, the nurse out there told me. Thursday. One o'clock, yeah. No problem. Hey, doc, can I try that coat on before I leave? I might wanna get me one of those. Hella cold at night, woooh, hella cold, you know?" She stood to go and headed for the coat.

Dr. Salim moved to usher her out of the exam room. "I have many, many more patients outside to test today, ma'am. Please. They are very cold, too."

"I just wanted to try on that coat, doc," Sascha replied, reaching out, but to no avail. The doctor blocked her way.

Dr. Salim slid open the accordion wall so Sascha could do nothing else but leave as she had been directed. As Sascha crossed through the Intake Room, where another homeless client waiting to get tested sat patiently with Judy, Dr. Salim called out.

"Don't forget, this Thursday!"

"Right, right, doc, one o'clock, I think I got it! Bye, Nurse Judy." Sascha walked out the side door of the mobile health van.

"Next, please come in!" Sascha heard as she walked away.

§ § §

"Judy, is there anyone else out there?"

"No one, Dr. Salim. Should we wait?"

"How many no-shows?"

Judy flipped through the intake assessment forms she and Dr. Salim completed on Tuesday. They were back in the mobile clinic van to do the follow-up readings.

"Lessee, looks like we're missing seven. Not bad, seven out of twenty-seven."

"Oh, I hate to waste those PPD injections, they're getting more expensive. Plus the wasted time, too. Let's just hold on a few more minutes, it is only just now 3:30."

"Don't forget we have to be at that office meeting by 4:00 sharp, which means we have to secure the van by no later than 3:50."

"I know, I know. Just another five or ten minutes."

Luckily, they waited for 12 minutes, because that's when Sascha walked up to the Intake Room door and poked her head in.

"Am I too late?"

"Yes," Judy said. "You are too late, but you're also very lucky. We waited for you."

"Sorry," Sascha said, climbing into the mobile van. "I got stuck downtown. Didn't have a bus ticket. Too far to walk and too scary to hitch. Thank the Lord some nice dude slipped me a transfer ticket! Woooh, I just made it."

"Name?" Judy asked.

"Coleman. Sascha Coleman."

"Coleman, Coleman... Coleman, Sascha! Okay, here, take this and head on back and give this to Dr. Salim." Judy handed Sascha her follow-up forms and off she went.

"Hi, doc. I'm back."

"Hmm, yes, I see. Barely made it, but here you are." Dr. Salim, her hands in the ever-present latex gloves, did not close the accordion wall this time. She motioned to the exam chair. "Sit, please."

Sascha immediately eyeballed Dr. Salim's winter coat, hanging on the hook in the corner. "Hey, there's that great coat again. 'Zit keeping you warm, doc?"

"Yes, it is. You and that coat! Here, I'll take your forms. Thanks." Dr. Salim slipped on a pair of reading glasses and took a quick look, checking off a couple of boxes.

The jacket had Sascha mesmerized, just hanging there as if it had not moved since last Tuesday, like it was just waiting for her. She spoke slowly, softly, like in some sort of trance. "You been using that coat, doc, or just leaving it on that hook to hold up the wall? Man, there's just something about that coat. Yeah, a girl would stay pretty warm in that coat, all right."

"Okay, forget the coat," Dr. Salim answered. "Let's have a look at your arm, please." She grabbed Sascha's hand again to pull her forearm closer. "Your hand is freezing! Are you okay?"

"Just cold out there, doc. Cold and getting colder from what everyone's been telling me."

"Yes, a cold front is here. You must be sure to get into a shelter tonight, be very sure."

Dr. Salim lowered her head to get a better look at the tested area on her arm, peering intently through the glasses that barely hung on to the tip of her nose. She pursed her lips, made a small 'hmmmph' sound, shrugged her shoulders ever so slightly, and nodded her head.

"Well, looks fine, there is no problem at all." Dr. Salim wrote a note on Sascha's test form, signed and dated it. Dr. Salim pulled the 2nd page copy from the two-page form. She handed Sascha the original top sheet.

"Okay, here you go. Take this to whomever you need to. Do you need any extra copies, Judy can get that for you?"

"Nah, doc, just the one is fine. Can I get one later if I need one?"

"Yes, yes, but you must call ahead or we will not have it on board. Do not just drop in. Call us first."

"Okay. Thanks." Sascha stood up and Dr. Salim did the same.

"Any chance I can try that coat on, doc, any chance at all? I just want to see how it fits and feels on me—I think it's my size."

"No, no, as a matter of fact we are running late for our next appointment at our office headquarters, so we have to go now, too, like you."

"Okay, doc, okay. I'm going."

Judy stood at the exit door, the stack of TB test reports and her planner clutched in her hands. "Come on, Sascha, time to go. Are you ready, Dr. Salim?"

"All right," Sascha said. "See you both, then."

"Take care, Sascha." Dr. Salim waved her out the door. "And stay warm!"

§ § §

In the middle of the clinical staff meeting, Barbara, the office receptionist, poked her head into the conference room.

"Francisco, the security officer from downstairs, and a city police officer are here. They said someone broke into the mobile clinic."

Dr. Salim hurriedly got up from her chair amid a worried exclamation from the group. "What? Come with me, Joseph and Judy. We'll see what's up."

Joseph was the other mobile clinic driver. He and Judy covered a number of duties on the clinical team, one being to secure the mobile clinics after serving homeless clients all day.

"Which van was broken into?" Judy asked. "I thought I made sure everything was locked up before we came up."

"My van didn't go out this afternoon, we just black-bagged a session at Salvation Army."

Barbara, like a seasoned civil servant, did not want to get too involved. "Uh, I didn't ask too many questions, so I don't know too much of the details. They're over in the front hallway for you."

The two officers were waiting for them.

Francisco knew them all by name. "Dr. Salim, Judy, Joe, this is Officer Warren from city police. Someone called in to the security desk downstairs to report they saw a person looking 'weird' around the vans." He motioned the quotation marks with two fingers from each hand. "I walked out to check on it, saw one of the van doors open and radioed CPD, per our security procedures."

"Hi, folks." Officer Warner nodded crisply to them. All business. "I received the call from City Dispatch about 20 minutes ago. When I arrived, the female that allegedly broke into your vehicle was talking to Francisco. He made her wait until I arrived."

Dr. Salim looked worried. "Where is the person now? Is she arrested? Did you let her go?"

"No, no," Francisco said. "She's downstairs, locked in my office."

Officer Warren spoke. "There was no one else in the vehicle. We would like you to see if anything has been stolen or broken. Are there any drugs or valuables kept on the vans? I did a quick walkthrough, but everything looks in order, as far as I can tell."

"Which van was broken into?" Judy asked again.

"The newer one," Francisco answered. "That's the one you two take out, right Judy, Dr. Salim?"

"Yes, right. But we keep nothing of value and we do not store any pharmaceuticals on the vans overnight, just for this reason." Dr. Salim thought for a moment. "There is a small microwave in both vans, though."

"And the phones and radios are left in there, too," Joseph offered.

"Well, could you come with me to be sure nothing was taken?"

They all hurried back to their desks momentarily to grab coats and put them on before heading down the stairs to the main floor. Officer Warren led the way and out through the back doors to the medical van. A quick inspection revealed nothing stolen or damaged.

"Francisco, what was the person doing when you stopped her?" Dr. Salim asked.

"Nothing, really, she was just backing out the door, getting ready to leave. I made her stop and wait for the Officer. She really didn't say anything to me, other than she was just trying to get out of the cold."

Salim continued. "Well, Officer, do we just let her go or what? It doesn't seem like anything's missing."

Judy nodded in agreement. "Everything looks fine."

Officer Warren said, "Why don't we all check with her again? Let's see if she reveals what she was doing or looking for. You might even know the person. I'll take all the info and file a police report, but if you decide not to press charges we'll just release her with a warning."

"Is it safe?" Judy asked.

"Oh yes, she's calm, not angry. Doesn't look like she's high or drunk or off in any way."

They followed Francisco next into the Security Office. To the right was his small office. He took out his set of keys, knocked softly, and then unlocked the door. Everyone but Judy filed into the small room. The culprit was sitting in the chair next to the metal desk.

"Ms. Coleman!" Dr. Salim recognized her immediately.

Sascha looked away for a moment and then brought her eyes back to Dr. Salim's. "Hey, doc. Howya doin'?"

17

Officer Warren, "So you know this person, Dr. Salim?"

Judy edged into the room. "Sascha Coleman. She was our last patient on the van today. A TB test. She was having her skin-test follow-up."

"Yes," Dr. Salim agreed. "That is right. Sascha Coleman."

"Ms. Coleman," Officer Warren looked at Sascha. "Is that true, you were on that van today?"

"Yes, sir, I was. But I needed another copy of my test report. I forgot to get one from the doc before. She said I could. I thought they still might be open."

"I told her she could get another copy, but not to just show up. Ms. Coleman needed to call first. Plus we are closed at that time."

Judy spoke up again. "Sascha knew we were closing the clinic for the day and must have known she was the last patient. When Sascha came in so late I told her she was lucky we waited so long for her to show up."

"Is that true, Ms. Coleman?"

"Nah, sir—guess I just forgot. I guess I figured they'd still be there and I could just get another copy."

"What did you need the other copy for?"

"Oh, well, you know, in case I lost the first copy."

"You mean the original," Dr. Salim said. "I gave you the original so you could use that one."

"Right, right. Yeah, I just wanted a copy."

"How did you get into the locked vehicle, ma'am?"

"It wasn't locked, sir. In fact, when I got there the door was open, so I peeked in. I thought the doc might be working in the back room so I went back there to see."

"Then what?" Officer Warren asked.

"We were all in a meeting upstairs," Dr. Salim told him.

"Then what did you do, Ms. Coleman?"

"Nothing, officer. No one was around so I just sat for a while. It was colder than hell outside and I just sat for a bit. I don't have a nice winter coat like the doc there, so I just stayed to warm up a bit. Nothing else. I didn't take anything or do anything."

"Any other questions, Dr. Salim? How about you, ma'am?"
Neither of them did.

"Okay, Ms. Coleman, please stay here for a minute. I'll be right back." He ushered Dr. Salim, Judy, and Francisco out of the office and shut the door behind him.

He faced them with his hands on his hips. "Doesn't look like anything else happened, other than her getting into the vehicle somehow. Do you want to pursue this any further? Anything else you want to do?"

"It is a bit unnerving that this happened," Dr. Salim said. "For some reason even more because she is one of our patients."

"What if she does this again? Or something worse?" Judy's voice sounded worried.

"You're positive the door was locked when you both left today?"

"I'm almost certain I locked up. I always do." Judy claimed.

"We are as sure as we can be, but of course we did not go back to double-check anything," Dr. Salim added. "It is normal procedure for us to lock-up each night after we close down. This has not happened on this van before."

"Well, I'll file the Police Report so we have something on record. I can't guarantee this will prevent it from happening in the future, but I'll let her know in no uncertain terms that if she does she will be taken in and prosecuted. I don't think she'll want that to happen."

"Okay," Dr. Salim agreed. "Please let us know if you need us for anything else."

"You also might want to be sure nothing of value is kept on the vehicles. And remind your staff to secure the vehicles each night. It wouldn't hurt to double check too, especially in times like these. You know this area isn't so great."

"Okay, thanks, Officer Warren. And thanks, Francisco, very much."

§ § §

When the phone rang, Dr. Salim was dreaming about defrosting a frozen chicken breast in the microwave at work. Very strange.

19

The phone rang again.

With a grunt, she reached over to turn on her bedside lamp. The clock radio across the room showed 4:20 a.m. She picked up the phone.

"Yes, Dr. Salim. Yes, yes. No. Of course, I will be there in about 30 minutes." Someone had broken into the office at work.

Dr. Salim dressed quickly, splashed cold water on her face and ran a brush quickly through her hair. She remembered that she had left her other coat at work so she pulled on a sweatshirt before heading out the door.

When Dr. Salim arrived, Francisco met her at the front entrance.

"The police have her in handcuffs, Dr. Salim. The alarm system went off around 4:00."

They hurried upstairs together to the program office.

"What happened, Francisco?" she asked him.

"It's that same lady. Copeland."

"You mean Coleman? The woman that broke into the medical van today—I mean yesterday?"

They entered the main office, the front lock and the doorframe obviously damaged. Officer Warren was there inside with another female officer. He introduced her as Officer Mesk.

"Yes, it's the same person, Dr. Salim. Sascha Coleman. We caught her back there. Francisco says that's your office."

"Yes, yes it is. Is everything all right?"

"Yes. She's the same as before. Calm. Seems straight. Will you please check the place over? Make sure nothing is damaged or out of place?"

"Where is she?"

"We've got her cuffed in our patrol car out front."

"What was she doing? Why is she doing this again?"

"She just keeps saying she's trying to stay out of the cold, trying to stay warm. She said to tell you—doc—that she's sorry."

"Sorry about what?"

"We don't know and she won't say. Maybe you can check things out and let us know. She just keeps saying that: 'Tell doc I'm sorry. I'm just cold. Tell doc I'm sorry.' Just like that."

Dr. Salim's walk through of the offices, including a thorough review of her own, showed nothing out of place. She did not notice anything missing at all.

"Well, we'll take her downtown and book her for breaking and entering."

"What will happen to her?"

"Probably nothing, unless she has prior arrests or an outstanding warrant. She'll stay the rest of the night in the lock-up and then be released later this morning, maybe noon. Like I said, she's just calm, not agitated or under the influence or anything."

"It is disturbing she decided to do this to our program, our office."

"Well, she'll be booked for it and this will be added to yesterday's incident."

"And then she'll be back on the street again."

"We'll make sure patrol spends a little more time and attention in this area. Could you please come down to confirm her identification for us?"

"Yes, I suppose, if I must."

"Thank you, doctor."

Dr. Salim could see the outline of Sascha Coleman in the side window as she approached the police car. The siren was off, but in the early morning light the glaring police lights still strobed brilliantly, obscenely. It felt surreal to Dr. Salim, like a scene in a movie.

It was just after 5:00 a.m., the coldest part of the morning, and Dr. Salim shivered in the frigid morning, her breath steaming from her nose and mouth. She realized the sweatshirt she put on in haste wasn't warm enough for this cold. Dr. Salim wrapped her arms tight around her chest and made a mental note to grab her winter coat from her office before leaving.

Officer Mesk led her to the patrol car's rear door. She opened it so Dr. Salim could take a look at the person inside. Sascha Coleman. A brief glance confirmed that.

"Yes, Officer, that is Sascha Coleman. She is the same person that broke into our medical clinic van earlier today—yesterday."

Sascha turned her head to see her. "Doc! Doc! I'm sorry, doc, I am. I'm just cold, doc. I'm sorry."

And that's when Dr. Salim noticed Sascha Coleman was wearing a very nice winter coat. Thick wool with a hood lined with white, soft fur. A hood you could cinch tightly to keep out the cold air.

Dr. Salim stepped up to the door. "You stole my coat? That's what you wanted all this time? My coat?"

"I tell you Doc! I'm sorry, doc, I am. I'm just cold, doc. I'm sorry."

Officer Mesk asked, "Is that your coat, Dr. Salim? Did she steal your coat?"

"Yes, it is, Officer. I think that is what she has wanted all this time."

"Doc! I'm sorry, doc. It's just so cold, doc. I'm sorry."

Officer Mesk pulled keys from her belt and reached into the police car. "Please remain still, Ms. Coleman."

"What are you doing, Officer?" Dr. Salim asked.

"I'm going to have her take off and return your coat," she replied without turning her head.

"No," Dr. Salim said. "Forget it. Please. Let her have it. She's right—it's very cold."

§ § §

Within the hour, Sascha had been driven to the police station, a statement taken, and fingerprinted. An officer took her in an elevator down to the jail rooms and her handcuffs removed. She was placed in a large holding cell, at least 50 feet long and 25 feet wide. A dozen or more women sat upright or sprawled about, some on benches along the walls, others on hard metal chairs. Most of them kept to themselves. One group of four women sat in one corner huddled together, laughing and talking in hushed whispers like they were actually enjoying themselves. There was an open toilet located in another back corner with a roll of toilet paper stuck on the floor next to it. No one sat near that area. The overhead florescent lights were all on and too bright.

The barred door of the cell opened automatically a few seconds

22

after they stepped up to it. The officer gently shoved Sascha in and the door shut with a loud clang behind her, locking her in with the rest.

Sascha sat herself down on an open bench. She pulled the winter coat tight around her body. The outside cold had worked its way down into the jails. Sascha took a quick glance around the room, then leaned her head back against the cement wall and closed her eyes.

She hadn't heard the four women approach her until one said, "I think that coat's my size, bitch."

Sascha opened one eye and saw them standing in front of her.

"What?" she mumbled.

"I said I think that coat's going to fit me just right, shit head."

"What—this coat?" Sascha replied.

"Give me that damn coat, bitch." The very large woman held out an extremely fat hand. A tattoo of a snake wound about her arm, from her wrist to her bicep, red blood dripping from the serpent's fanged mouth. She was wearing hot pink-rimmed sunglasses. "Give it to me or I'm taking it."

Sascha took another look at the woman and the three crowded behind her in forceful unity. She slowly took off the coat, then rolled it into a ball and tossed it to the woman. "Here," she said flippantly. "Take the dang, raggedy thing. It ain't keeping me warm anyway."

Then she closed her eyes again and feigned sleep until she heard the group laugh and shuffle back to their spot in the back corner. Sascha pulled her arms tighter across her chest and tried to stay warm.

GARBAGE SOUP

Based on the fable "Stone Soup": Three hungry soldiers set up camp in the town square of an impoverished village. They boil water in a large cauldron and explain to the curious and hungry villagers that they have a magic stone that will make a wonderful soup for their dinner. Oh, but if only they had a bit of onion or carrot or meat the soup would be even more luscious, the soldiers tell the villagers! Each of the villagers offers a small contribution to the soup pot in exchange for a bowl of soup. Together, they create a soup that becomes a feast for all.

The moral of the fable is: By working together a greater good can be achieved.

W e should stop here, Mommy."

"Well, it's as good a place as any." The woman sighed, peering over the girl's uncovered head to take a look around. Lord, she was getting taller every day!

The sun was starting to go down. Only a few golden rays reached where they stood. It was dark and shadowy under the freeway overpass, but there weren't too many cars on the road and it was the rush hour. That was a good sign. Most likely there would be even less traffic later that night. And that meant less noise, fewer bothersome lights.

Dust floated down over the edge of the overpass, shimmering briefly in the last of the fading light. Maybe they would have a peaceful night's rest. That hadn't always been the case over the last six months, so she was grateful. Who could have imagined such a simple, little thing—like a quiet night of sleep—would mean so much to them?

The woman felt the beginning of the evening chill in the air. With a weary sigh, she reached down to tuck the bottom of the hooded sweatshirt into her faded jeans and pulled the down jacket's Velcro strap tighter around her neck to keep out the coming cold. Along with the long johns under her pants, thick socks, hiking boots, green wool cap hiding her ears and long brown hair, she was in full outdoor garb. These were some of the last clothes she still held onto from "before".

Before the divorce, the anger, the legal battles and legal fees, the tears, the short-lived studio apartment, and the pain. Before she and Rose ended up on the street.

The last time she wore these clothes they most likely were camping and having a good time. It was probably at Big Sur, which was one of their favorite spots. How ironic, she thought, back then being out-doors meant they were on vacation! That seemed like a long, long time ago—another lifetime. Now Lydia wore the outfit all the time, the growing number of dirty spots proved that. For some reason she was always cold now, always.

Lydia stole a glance at her daughter, Rose. A blue denim jacket over her grey hooded sweatshirt, the faded jeans and black street boots made Rose look just like any other teenager in the world. Her medium length strawberry blond hair was tucked into a red, knitted scarf draped around her neck. No make-up, but Rose's cheeks were a healthy pink color. The girl didn't need the make-up anymore anyway. Rose wasn't much different from any other kid, she just happened to be living on the street with her mother.

At that thought, Lydia felt a moment of deep sadness. The sadness quickly became a pang of desperation and then the sudden flash of the dangerous precipice to losing total control. With silent resolve she suppressed those feelings again, and did so almost before the thought registered in her mind about needing to do so. No, she couldn't afford to lose control, not again, not ever. What would become of Rose? Of them? And in her heart of hearts Lydia really did believe that some-day things would work out, really—it was just that "someday" was taking much longer than expected.

"Are you hungry, baby?" Lydia asked Rose, caressing her cheek with a grimy hand. There was dirt under every fingernail. Once upon a time they were polished and colored. But now the polish remaining was dull shards of jagged, rust-colored streaks.

"Yes, momma, I am sorta hungry tonight," the young girl replied, resting her cheek softly against her mother's cold touch. She reached up and covered her mother's hands with her own. Neither of them had eaten much over the last three days and her empty stomach proved that.

"Let's do the soup tonight, see how that comes out. If it works, that ought to fill us right up and take away the chill. Come on, let's."

Lydia pushed the shopping cart deeper into the shadows and stopped at a large metal garbage can standing away from the concrete wall of the overpass. Weak entrails of gray smoke seeped from the top and swirled away.

Rose peered inside the can, keeping her hands back to avoid contact with the potentially hot metal. Bright red embers smoldered amid the blackened, charred wood and melted, but still recognizable, aluminum cans and broken glass. A partially melted doll's head somehow survived the last fire, a tiny patch of red, curly hair still attached in defiance. Half of the doll's bright red smile gaped sickly from the distorted face.

"Somebody's fire," Lydia claimed.

She pointed to a jumble of garbage bags and a few pieces of folded cardboard a few feet away. A dirty, plastic milk carton half-filled with liquid, water maybe, and a short stack of yellowed newspapers stood amongst the tied bags. "Looks like their stuff is still here. They'll be back."

Rose moved away from the garbage can. She scanned the area. "There's a lot of other stuff around here, too. I bet there'll be plenty of folks here later."

The woman nodded; Rose was probably right. Lydia picked out the piles of junk scattered about. *Well*, she chuckled to herself, *what most people would think were piles of junk*. These things were the few and precious belongings of the homeless, the transient, the needy, the hobos, bums, whatever the nom de jour was for them. She identified these belongings right away—she pushed her own about all day, her things and Rose's.

The two moved further under the concrete structure, finally picking a fairly clear area just about in the middle of the overpass. Here they parked their shopping cart.

At least five other makeshift resting spots—Rose liked to call them nests—were positioned around them. Close, but not too close. Other nests were strewn about. Most had the requisite plastic milk jug for drinking water and stacks of newspaper. Not that most of these folks really kept up with current events, but newspaper was a good insulator for thin pants and torn coats. It also slowed water from leaking into used, holey shoes for a little while. Some of them had blankets, folded up for the most part. Lydia was fairly surprised these were left un-attended and hoped that meant these folks were trusting, and prayed that they were also kind. Many of these things could be easily obtained from recycle bins and garbage cans, but sometimes it was a whole lot easier to just take them from your neighbor.

Rose was right. There would be a number of other homeless folks to keep them company, maybe share soup with tonight.

Lydia and Rose began the now familiar task of clearing debris from their spot, moving small rocks, bits of broken glass away in silence. Each had their assigned tasks, learned well from daily experience over their homeless travels. Lydia pulled a folded piece of cardboard from the bottom section of the cart. Once a packing crate for a bookshelf, the cardboard was thick and still intact, even though it had been used many times and the creases from the folds were torn in a few places.

She handed the cardboard to Rose, who unfolded it on the ground. Lydia then removed a blue moving tarpaulin from the cart and spread that over the box. It was her prized possession! A month ago, during a late summer rain, she forced herself to ask two men waiting out the rain in the back of an almost empty moving van if they had an old tarp she could have. They never said a word, but just handed over a tarp. Since then, Lydia and Rose put the thick, quilt-like, moving tarp to good use, especially as the fall, with its dark, cold nights, came upon them quickly. Lydia vowed to protect this tarp with her life. She knew it protected theirs.

"Rose, you better start looking for some wood to get the fire going. We want to be sure the blaze is nice and warm before sunset." Lydia again scanned the area. "And keep a look out for a can we might use for the soup."

Rose set off through the temporary nests and scraggly brush of the homeless site. She had done this many times over the last few months and, each time, luck had been on her side. But since a number of other people already set up residence at this spot, wood scraps for a fire might be hard to come by. She might have to do a bit of walking to find enough. Yet, she felt good and hopeful about the thought of soup, and fully expected things would work out okay.

Ah, the soup! Just the mention of the soup awoke great hunger pangs in both of them. And of course the soup was always a great adventure for them, too! A mystery story, with neither able to guess the outcome until the drama played out. Sometimes the outcome miraculously appeared, as Rose liked to put it, and they might spend a luxurious evening in their outdoor campsite with newfound friends. Other nights they went to bed with their hunger pangs and the echo of jeers and threats to keep them company, a reminder of the hard life they would awaken to in the morning. The play always had a surprise ending, sometimes good, but not always. What would happen this time?

Against the wall of the overpass, Lydia found a number of large stones, most likely cleared away from some of the sites. Turning back to retrieve her shopping cart that was still laden with a number of their belongings, she returned and placed two of the larger stones gently on top. Lydia wheeled back to the site chosen for the night.

For a good half-hour, Lydia went back and forth, setting more large stones into a circular pattern near their nest. The center of the pattern was large enough for a nice fire and the stones tall enough to prop the soup can on for cooking, once they found one. She promised herself, again, that one of these days she would try to get hold of a large pot so they wouldn't have to scrounge around for one all of the time.

When Lydia was satisfied with her stone fire circle, she got up and searched about for water. A faucet had to be nearby, what with everyone else's water jugs, and soon found one leading from the end of the overpass structure. She squatted down to get a better look. The handle was missing but someone affixed a rusty old pipe wrench to the end with black electrician's tape. Half of that handle had broken off, but there was still enough to turn the water on. About six inches of old black hose connected to the spigot. Lydia straightened up to see if Rose had come back.

There was her daughter, dragging a large tree branch behind her. The branch wasn't very thick, but still had a number of small, thin arms shooting off the main stem. On these Rose laid a piece of cardboard. On top rode the bits and pieces of wood she managed to find. Rose also stumbled upon part of a pallet crate, which still had a few fairly large pieces of wood to burn, although they would have to somehow find a way to pry them apart.

Lydia wasn't sure if this would be enough firewood for the soup, but they were still lucky to have found this much. The magic of the soup would have to do for the rest. She watched Rose drag the entire load to their nest.

"Fantastic, Rose," Lydia exclaimed, as she began piling the wood next to the fire circle. "See if you can break some of these small branches up. Use the big branch to pry apart the pallet. Just place the thicker end between the boards, keep your weight on the other end, and push down—that should work. I think I saw a can back up the road as we passed—I'll go check it out."

As she walked away, Lydia shrugged, still thinking about how nice it would be to own a large soup pot to use. Unless by some crazy chance they were very, very lucky, that wasn't likely to happen. Still, they always managed to find a trash can clean enough for the soup. In fact, cleaning out the can had become a major part of making the soup, the start of the whole drama. Act 1.

There were a few garbage cans under the overpass, but most of these either had been used for making a fire the night before, evidenced by the smoke seeping out of them, or were too rusted and dirty to use for the soup. Lydia pushed her cart back along the short path she and Rose used earlier. Stepping from the shadows of the overpass, she noticed two men leaning against the side of the rising concrete structure, almost hidden by a small Manzanita bush.

One was asleep, his arms folded across his chest. His tattered blue coat was partially unzipped and revealed a dirty, hooded sweatshirt beneath. An empty pint bottle lay next to him in the dirt. His right hand was wrapped in a soiled ace bandage held together with a large silver safety pin. If it was there to help keep a wound clean, the wrap was no longer doing its job.

The other man wore a greasy San Francisco Giants baseball cap. A scraggly, peppery beard covered the lower half of his face. He stared at her and took a long pull from a cigarette. Lydia caught his eye as she passed and slowed momentarily.

"I'm looking for a nice garbage can. I want to make some hot soup for the cold night ahead. There's nothing like hot soup to warm a person's soul up." Lydia nodded and smiled as she spoke to the smoking man, then moved on without waiting for a reply.

Lydia pushed her grocery cart further ahead, finally coming upon the can she spotted earlier, hoping with all hope that the can would be good enough to use. She didn't want to spend a lot of time searching — night was already fast approaching. If it became too dark it would be impossible to find a good can at all and they would have to give up on the soup for tonight. But Lydia had a good feeling about this night.

The garbage can looked pretty good on the outside. It was lying on its side, partially covered by a few pages of brittle yellow newspaper. A pile of dry leaves spilled out of the open end. Lydia kicked the newspaper away and lifted the bottom end of the can, spilling its contents onto the ground. Nothing but more leaves, paper, a couple of plastic soda bottles, dirt, and dust.

She set the can back upright and peered in. A quick smile crossed her lips when she saw the can looked fairly clean inside. Thankfully there wasn't any moldy garbage or dead rodents, covered in maggots or other bugs, like the one they found the last time they tried to make the soup. Even the outside appeared in good shape, rust kept away by a thick layer of dark red paint covering the lower half of the metal can.

Nope, this will do just fine, she thought to herself.

Lydia pushed her cart against the can and jammed a couple of rocks against the back wheels to hold the cart steady. Bending down to lift the empty can, she almost lost control as it slipped against the edge of the metal cart. By shifting her weight just so Lydia was able to flop the can into the cart, top-side down. The bottom half stuck up, but she only had a little ways to go to bring it back to their site. Lydia saw it was in really good condition: very little rust, if any, and no holes—perfect to withstand the fire's heat and hold in the soup!

Lydia whistled, mostly air, as she returned to the site with the soup pot. The night was shaping up well. This time when Lydia passed the two lounging men, both of them were smoking.

"Whatcha got there?" the man who had been asleep earlier asked her. She stopped to answer.

"I've got me a fine soup pot," Lydia replied.

"Soup pot?" he exclaimed. "Looks like a garbage can to me. I can't rightly recall the last time I had me a good bowl of soup out of a trash can. Can you, Jack? When was that—our last prime rib dinner at Le Soupa de Trash Can?"

He poked his partner in the ribs with his bandaged hand, gave a loud laugh and winked at Lydia, flashing a smile that was missing a large front tooth.

"Yes," Lydia replied, stroking the bottom of the can. "It's a garbage can now, but after my daughter and I clean it all out and get it good and hot, we'll make our world famous home-cooked soup in it. Once you've smelled the fragrant soup you'll forget all about this being a garbage can! And if you taste the hot soup you'll think you're sitting and eating right in the middle of the dining room of the finest restaurant in town."

With that, Lydia moved on again without waiting for another reply. The men's gazes weighed on her back as she pushed her cart and soup pot away.

Heading back to Rose, Lydia noticed a few more people had returned back to their nests, including children as well. Most stood or sat around while others were getting ready for the evening, spreading out cardboard, blankets, and putting sweaters and coats on. All of these people noticed her and her strange collection as she passed by, but few said anything to her. To the ones that did ask, Lydia gave the same reply or explanation. The can was just a garbage can now, but wait until the wonderful hot and fragrant soup was made. Of course, some of the children just couldn't let her pass without a few questions and smiles and giggles.

"What's the garbage can for? What's your name? How are you going to make soup in that thing? What kind of soup, chicken noodle or—ugh!—tomato? How can you make soup in a garbage can—are you magical?"

For these children, Lydia stopped and let them gather around her. Then she placed her hands on the garbage can sitting in her grocery cart, stroking and petting it as if it was a very special object come to life. The finest soup pot in the world. In a voice loud enough so not only the kids could hear but also any adult listening in on their conversation, as most of them were, she patiently answered every one of their questions.

"Yes, this will be a very special soup and to be cooked in this very special soup pot. But first, Rose and I will need to clean this can up and scrub all of the dirt out so our soup will be hot and wonderful. It will smell like the best soup you've ever smelled before and will taste like no other soup you've ever tasted. And when you sleep tonight, your dreams will be filled with the smell and taste of the soup, just like your full bellies will be."

Her responses elicited more questions from the children.

"What kind of soup is it? How will you eat the soup? Will we get to have some soup?" Again, Lydia answered, her voice loud and clear.

"Rose and I don't know what kind of soup we will make yet. We never know until it's all cooked. We do have some special things to put into it, you'll see! And we'll eat ours with a bowl and a spoon. How will you eat yours? We'll be making a great big pot of soup, so perhaps there will be plenty if you should like to share it with us. But now I have to go or we won't have time to make the soup!"

And this time she pushed on, back to Rose and their site. Some of the children followed, chattering quietly, but excitedly, behind her.

Rose stacked all of the wood she brought back, including the pallet board pieces she separated. The stack was pretty high—at least high enough to build a hot fire to heat the water, surely enough to get it boiling.

"Come on, Rosie," Lydia said to her when she stepped up with the cart and can. "Come with me to start cleaning this pot. Hopefully we can get some of these kids to help."

Together the two of them pushed the cart and 'soup pot' back over to the faucet Lydia located earlier.

Lydia turned the spigot on and wet down the outside of the can first. Using old rags, the two of them scrubbed good and hard. Much of the dirt and grime came off with each swipe. The caked on patches took a good deal more muscle, but with time the outside of the garbage can began to look much better.

A group of about a half dozen children came over to watch them, soon followed by a smaller group of adults.

Rose smiled a "Hi all!" at the kids and Lydia gave just a smile and a grunt to the adults. Neither of them stopped cleaning the can, however. Finally, one of the young boys came up and asked if he could help.

"Why do you want to help?" Rose asked him, loudly enough for all to hear. "You don't even know what we're doing."

She reached deep into the can to clean out more of the dirt. Lydia rinsed out the spot Rose just swiped.

"What ARE you doing?" one of the adults asked, as Lydia threw the boy a rag.

"Why, we're cleaning this-here soup pot for tonight," Lydia answered, sweeping her hair away from her face. "Use that rag to help clean up this pot, boy, and you can share in the soup tonight, IF you're allowed to."

The young boy looked over at a woman standing in the group nearby. His silent plea was answered with a quick nod. He smiled and began to help Rose rub down the can.

"Soup, in a garbage can?" another adult inquired. "I'm not sure if that's a very good idea."

"You eat soup out of a pot, don't you?" Lydia asked him. "Well, once we get this can clean enough it will be the best and biggest soup pot in the county." She smiled at the boy helping them. "Good job, son, you're really cleaning that can up good. The soup's going to be extra savory tonight!"

"What kind of soup are you making?" a woman asked, the boy's mother.

"GARBAGE SOUP!" Lydia and Rose yelled with delight at the same time. "Great garbage soup!!!"

"Oooooooh!" The kids laughed and squealed. "We're not eating garbage soup!"

"Sounds a bit off," the woman replied.

"It's not really garbage soup because we use garbage," Rose explained. "We call it garbage soup because we use a special, cleaned out garbage can for our soup pot."

"It's really the best soup I've ever tasted," smiled Lydia, closing her eyes as if she were dreaming about the soup. "It tastes so wonderful, and it's good and hot, and the smells just enter your nose and fill-up your whole body! It will be the best soup you've ever tasted, too, you'll see if you share it with us!"

"Well, what's really in it?" Another man asked.

By that time, two other kids slipped in to help clean while Rose stood back and rinsed. Lydia was now free to face the group gathered 'round and answer their questions.

"You know, that's the funny part," Lydia replied. "The soup's never come out the same way twice. But it's always the best soup we've ever had. What do you like in your soup?"

"Hmmm, well, I like a bit of onion and ham in mine," the man replied. And you could tell by his wistful tone and the gleam in his eyes he was picturing a big, hot, steamy bowl of soup, flavored with bits of ham and chopped onion. "And maybe some celery!"

"That sounds good alright," Lydia responded. "I don't think we have any ham or onion OR celery tonight. But if YOU have any of that why don't you bring it on over and we'll add it to the pot and you can share it with us. It's going to be great!"

"Well," the man said. "I do have a bit of sliced ham from a sandwich I got over behind the deli today, but I was going to share that with my boy there tonight."

"Don't think about it for another second," Lydia replied, clapping him good-naturedly on the shoulder. "Bring the boy too, there'll be plenty! Just bring your ham sandwich and a big bowl over in about an hour and we'll add it right to the soup. That ham will add great flavor and the bread can serve to help thicken it up. And don't forget your spoons!"

"There's tomato in that sandwich, too!" The man said, smacking his lips joyfully.

"Even better!" Lydia smiled. "We'll add it all!"

"Add it all to what?" Another man spoke up.

It was the sleeping man with the bandaged hand, come over to check out the newcomers and their crazy soup. He glanced over at the folk gathering around Rose and Lydia and the garbage can. Or was that a soup pot? The man shook his head at Lydia to let her know he thought the whole idea was wacko.

"Sounds like all you got so far is half a ham sandwich and a dirty old garbage can. Please tell me and everyone else around here how that becomes the greatest soup ever made?"

He looked again at all the others, trying to get them to join him in his disbelief.

"Well, first of all, take a look at that dirty old garbage can." Lydia pointed back at the cleaning kids. She called to Rose, "Rose, stand that pot up and rinse it off so these folks can see our newest soup pot!"

Rose did as Lydia asked and with one final splash of water on the outside of the can she rinsed the last bit of dirt away. The garbage can was much cleaner than before. Maybe even clean enough to make soup in it!

"Now see, sir, you thought this pot wasn't going to work out, but it sure has become a great soup pot, don't you think?! Imagine that pot filled with hot, thick flavorful soup! Won't that take the chill from the night air tonight?!" Lydia eyed the man with a smile. "And, of course, we hope you can come share it with us?"

"Well," the man replied. "I'm not sure what you and your kid are, well, cooking up, so to say. Well, I don't know, but, aw what the hell, that can maybe WOULD make a great mess of soup. But I don't really have much to add to it."

"Anything you have will help. Every little bit adds flavor to a great pot of soup!" Lydia told him and the others around her nodded in agreement. "What exactly DO you have to add to the soup?"

"Let's see," the man thought out loud, scratching his head with his bandaged hand. "I have a half a bag of potato chips, barbecue, and most of a green salad from Wendy's. You think that will help?"

"Will that help?" Lydia exclaimed. "My-oh-my! That, added to the ham sandwich, added to the greatest hot and steaming pot of soup ever cooked will be great! Can you just imagine how thick the soup will get from those chips and how the salt and barbecue seasonings will flavor the savory broth? And the veggies from the salad will add even more flavor and fiber and vitamins and all that good stuff that we all need."

The man's gap-toothed smile showed he had changed his mind. "Well, I guess my friend Jack might have something to throw in, too, if that's okay with you two."

With a nod and a smile back from Lydia, he went off to retrieve his treasures.

"This soup is going to be the best batch yet!" Rose expressed with glee. "What about you other kids, do you all want to share soup with us tonight? It's such a great big pot we'll have enough to feed a whole city! We'll eat soup 'til we burst!"

"Hey, I think we have a box of leftover Kentucky Fried Chicken. We can add that, can't we?"

"Sam, you better ask mom before you promise that! That was supposed to be for our supper."

"Well, now we can have wonderful, hot soup and THAT can be our supper. I'm gonna go ask her right now." Sam threw down his cleaning rag and ran off to ask his mom.

"Mmmmm, chicken would make the soup almost too good to be true. That, plus all of the salad veggies, ham, tomato, and the barbecue potato chips. I can almost taste it already!" Lydia closed her eyes and licked her lips. "Come on, Rose, let's get this clean soup pot over to the fire and get it filled with water to boil!"

"Well, now, here ma'am," the man with the sandwich cut in. "Please let me and a few of the guys here carry this heavy soup pot over to your fire. And some of you kids, start filling your buckets and jugs with water to fill up this pot once it's set in place!"

"And don't forget." Lydia called out just as everyone started to move. "Let's all share in the soup tonight! So bring your best bowl and your biggest spoon when the soup's done. And bring whatever you have to add to the pot as soon as you can so all of the flavors can cook and bubble and meld together while the soup starts getting hot! In about an hour or so we're going to have the greatest pot of soup ever made, I swear I'm sure about that!"

Soon the men placed the soup pot atop the circle of firestones. Many jugs and buckets of water later, the pot was about two-thirds full of water. More than enough to feed all of the people now congregated under the freeway overpass for the night, PLUS any friends that stopped by!

There were at least fifteen adults in the makeshift campground and another ten children. Most had by now set-up their nests for the evening, spreading cardboard and blankets around, bundling up in sweatshirts and coats, getting ready to eat whatever meager supplies they had for dinner. Most usually had very little to eat.

But that night, there was a different feeling running through the camp: a different smell, a tingle—and all because of the soup! People who wouldn't normally have a word to say to one another were now talking about the soup, what was in it, what they were going to add to it, how good it was going to be. Each of them had a different, special version of the soup in their mind, perhaps some remembrance of steaming hot soup filling a small hungry belly, of sitting around the table with family and friends, of home. They each smiled when they thought of that soup.

So, it was no problem for each of them to find some small tidbit, some morsel, some leftover to add to the pot. They would all share and there would be more than enough for everyone!

Lydia and Rose started the fire under the pot with small broken branches, bits of scrap wood, and wadded up strips of newspaper. When the smaller kindling caught fire, they carefully added larger branches and a few of the pallet board pieces, saving enough to keep the fire going for some time.

The bandaged man's friend, Jack, came along and added to the woodpile, asking humbly if his contribution was enough so that he could share in the soup as well. After talking to Lydia for a minute, she also discovered he had half a bag of carrots wrapped up in his blanket. That, too, went into the pot, cut up into scrumptious chunks.

Eventually, one by one, all of the adults came over, some with their children tagging along shyly, adding whatever they were able. While smiling and talking gaily with Rose and Lydia they added so many things!

One woman had a bag of French fries from Burger King. Another had a large onion that was quickly chopped and added. One family of four brought over a plastic baggie full of leftover spaghetti from a free lunch they received behind a café that afternoon. The ham sandwich went in, as did the salad and chips. A small cheer went up throughout the camp as the box of half-eaten Kentucky Fried Chicken was ceremoniously dumped into the pot!

Rose pulled a very large wooden spoon from somewhere within their cart of belongings, almost big enough to be called a paddle, which they used a few times before to stir soup. It had a long handle that could reach down into the belly of the pot and a thick round head to stir all of the soup fixings. She made a great show of presenting the spoon to Lydia, who, in turn, solemnly dipped the spoon into the pot and began a slow, even stirring.

She smiled at everyone and called, "Soup's on!" Many of the adults, and all of the kids, clapped with glee.

First, a faint wisp of steam floated off the top of the liquid. Then, a few minutes later, tiny little bubbles formed on the outside ring of the soup, close along the edge of the soup pot. The bubbles began to get a little bit bigger and more steam rose off the soup! The cooking process was luxuriously slow and the anticipation wonderful! More wood was placed under the pot and into the fire.

And as the soup began bubbling even stronger, more people came over to add to the pot.

Three potatoes were diced and dropped in next. A man dug into his pockets and pulled out a handful of salt, pepper and ketchup packets which he opened and added. He threw the empty packets into the fire, causing it to sparkle brightly to match their own growing excitement. A young man offered a defrosted bag of peas and carrots and emptied these contents into the soup pot. He smiled at Rose shyly, and then walked back into the shadows, backing out of the fire's glare. Another man gently opened the plastic top of a small Tupperware bowl and three-bean salad tumbled into the pot, kidney beans and green beans and garbanzo beans, all in a thick Italian dressing. Lydia gave the man a quick hug for this treasure and he proudly stepped back smiling, joining in with the others now milling about the soup pot.

Every once in a while someone would take a step closer to the pot, adult and child alike, to peer over the edge, take a quick look in, and breathe in the deep smell of the broth. Then they would smile at Rose or Lydia, giggle and shrug their shoulders, at once sheepish and excited, and quickly slide back into the group, where they joined in the conversation about soup.

Because that's what everyone was talking about: soup!

They talked about recipes for fantastic bowls of soup and the great smells of so many different soups. Some spoke about how good soup was for you. Others reminisced about sitting around having soup with family and friends. All of them agreed nothing felt better than a cold body filling up on a bowl of good, hot, soup. For a little while, with the pot bubbling away, melding all of the different, individual ingredients they all added into a thicker, richer, more flavorful soup — their dinner! — they forgot about their homelessness, their needs, their fears, and were cheered.

And how was the soup coming?

"Oh, it's going to be soup in just a little while!" Lydia called out, still stirring the pot contents gently. "It's hot and getting thicker and starting to smell soooo good. Come and smell and see!"

They all did, gathering even closer, taking a peek, stealing a whiff. It was all so good!

And still more came to add to the soup. Here was a pack of hot dogs, cut into small chunks. A woman dropped in a bag of pre-cut cabbage originally intended for coleslaw. This one added two whole tomatoes. Then, an older gentleman walked up with a small parcel in brown plain paper.

"I was going to feed this to the dog," he mumbled, opening the package. Inside was a savory ham bone with small chunks of ham still clinging to the bone. He lowered it into the soup and a resounding cheer erupted from the gathering. Men and women shook his hands and patted him on the back. Lydia even gave him a small peck on the cheek, which startled him while his eyes shone bright.

"Now, we just have to cook this for a while," Lydia exclaimed with a big smile. "And when it's done, everyone better get in line and bring your biggest bowl, because there's enough soup here for an army. What a great soup dinner we will all have tonight!"

By then, everyone had added something and all were ready to partake in the hot soup when Lydia told them it was ready. Everyone could tell from the thickness of the broth and the smells that the soup truly was going to be the best soup they had ever had!

So they waited and talked and smiled to each other, kindred souls for at least one night, one night of shared soup.

Some of the kids raced around the campsite, too happy and excited to keep still. Someone had opened a few cans of warm beer and these were being passed amongst some of the adults. Conversation and laughter grew. Some of the adults even began an impromptu dance along the edge of the cooking fire. Lydia clapped her hands in time against the stirring spoon. Rose joined in, dancing happily with the shy young man who had contributed the bag of peas and carrots. These folks hadn't shared such sounds of delight and feeling of happiness for some time and definitely never in this makeshift homeless camp.

Lydia and Rose's eye met as mother stirred and daughter danced. They smiled knowingly at each other and their smiles reached out deeply for one another. They knew the soup magic worked again and they honestly believed this was going to be the best soup ever made. They couldn't wait to serve it up and to eat their fill along with all of the others.

"Okay, everybody," Lydia called out again above the noise and frivolity. "I'm going to taste the soup and see if it's ready!"

Everyone gathered even closer around Lydia and the pot. She brought the large wooden spoon out of the soup pot, tapping it loudly against the side, like a drum, until she could feel everyone bursting with anticipation. Then she slowly dipped the spoon into the boiling soup and, grasping in strongly with both hands, brought it back up slowly to her lips.

Lydia smiled then blew onto the spoon. With a momentary glance at everyone as they shuffled ever more tightly around the hot pot of soup, she tipped the spoon into her mouth, closed her eyes and swallowed. Lydia's smile grew. Then, her eyes flew open wide and she laughed out:

"SOUP'S ON, EVERYBODY!"

And just at that same exact moment brilliant, bright lights flashed from the overpass, settling on the group gathered near the fire.

Four police cars and a police van swung off the overpass in unison, with loud, metallic crunches as each vehicle popped up over the curb. The cars rambled down the short embankment and through the campsite, quickly swinging around the group of homeless people and surrounding them and their cooking fire. The headlights from the vehicles were glaring and hideous. Flashing police lights from two of the squad cars turned on, rotating and creating an almost alien atmosphere.

The people of the encampment instinctively huddled together, trying to do so while avoiding the fire and the hot can.

Police in riot gear descended from all of the vehicles.

One clicked on a megaphone and, directing his booming voice at the crowd, yelled, "THIS IS A RESTRICTED AREA. YOU ARE ORDERED TO

EXIT FROM THIS CITY AREA IMMEDIATELY. WE HAVE WARNED YOU BEFORE. PLEASE LEAVE THIS AREA IMMEDIATELY."

The policemen moved in, pushing the people away from the fire and separating them from one another. They grunted and swore as they drove the people away, poking some with their riot clubs to move them along.

An older man, the one who offered the succulent ham bone, was pushed a little too roughly and he tripped and fell to his knees. This prompted one of the officers to kick him in the ribcage with a heavy boot. The fallen man grunted, but heaved himself up before another blow could come his way. He scrambled off, clutching his side.

All of the others scattered in confusion.

Again the officer with the megaphone commanded, "MOVE OUT QUICKLY. NOW. THIS IS NOT A PUBLIC CAMPING LOCATION. MOVE OUT OR YOU WILL BE TAKEN INTO CUSTODY FOR TRESPASSING. MOVE OUT."

The officer walked up to the bubbling pot of soup. The large spoon was forgotten in the pot when Lydia and Rose were hustled off with the rest of their homeless friends. The officer grabbed the spoon handle, dipped the head into the hot, thick soup, and brought the spoon up to his nose for a smell. He breathed deeply. In disgust, he threw the spoon and its contents onto the ground. The treasured spoon split right down the middle and broke into two perfectly equal halves.

"What the hell is this?" The officer barked in revulsion. "Did they make this crap out of garbage?"

The officer raised his right boot onto the tip of the hot garbage can and shoved with all of his might. The can and its contents came crashing to the ground. Thick, luxurious soup spilled into the fire where it bubbled and boiled briefly, sending thick wafts of rich-smelling steam up into the night air, until the cooking fire smothered out. The campsite would have been pitch-black if not for the flashlights of the police officers and the grotesque, swirling headlights from the police cars.

§§§

Later that night, two dark figures walked into the dark, quiet clearing under the overpass.

One of them, a woman, pushed a cart full of personal possessions to the spot where the cooking fire had been. She stopped at the garbage can, once full of hot soup, now lying on its side in dirt and mud. Sighing, she grabbed the collars of her dirty down jacket with her grimy hands and pulled the Velcro straps together tighter. The night grew suddenly much, much colder.

She reached into her cart and after a brief moment pulled out a large, wooden bowl. In quiet dignity she knelt and, using her hands, began to scrape up soup ingredients puddled along the inside of the can and also on the ground at the can's lip. The other, a younger woman in a knitted scarf, stooped and began to pick up small morsels in the dark.

As they gathered up these scraps, the older woman found the ham bone still with bits of gristle, fat and meat clinging to the bone. She tenderly wiped dirt and grime from it before placing the bone in her soup bowl. Tears filled her eyes as the bowl slowly filled.

She moved on her knees back to the can. The young one held the large bowl securely on the ground near the lip of the cold garbage can. The other moved to the back end and gently lifted, pouring the last remaining trickle of soup into the bowl.

At least Rose would have something to eat tonight.

SHOE GOD

Based on the fable "The Hares and the Frogs": Once more faced with impending danger and running for their lives, the hares decide to end their continuous fear by jumping off a precipice into the deep lake below. But, just as the hares are about to jump, dozens of frogs lying on the banks below are startled by the noise of the hares' large feet and the frogs take off helter-skelter for safety in the deepest part of the lake. The hares realize that the frogs are even more afraid than they are.

The moral of the fable is: There is always someone worse off than you.

Andre stopped with his back against the cement wall. He stood for a moment, hiding in the last available bit of moon-shadow before making his way across the street to the park. He peered into the darkness between the park's bushes, wanting to make sure the homeless guy was still sleeping there.

It wasn't too hard to tell the dude was there since he could hear the guy's loud snoring even from across the street, ripping through the usual sounds of the night. Still, in the distance Andre could hear a city bus making a final late night run down 53rd Ave. and a small dog yipping at something unfamiliar in the dark. He also noticed a couple of other street guys sitting on a park bench nearby, sipping from the small, dark bottle they passed and muttering about something only they cared about.

Andre liked this time of night. For some reason, he trusted it. Or maybe he trusted himself in it. He felt safe, invisible, with the freedom to do what he wanted without anyone criticizing him. He squinted. Yeah, the guy was there. Good.

Andre grabbed the pair of Nikes draped over his shoulder, one last look before dropping them off. Damn, these were some killer shoes, just the right size for him, too. Size 11.

Nike AirMax, black with the royal blue heel. Sweet. But not for him, no, his parents made that pretty freakin' crystal clear. What, $155, how could they not afford that?! There was no reason they couldn't, not really. It was all crap. Whatever. Let them make up reasons: his schoolwork, his grades, his attitude, his behavior. Screw that. Big effin' deal, he knew how to get what he wanted anyway. So what if he couldn't keep them? At least he got them, had them. Now dang it, no thanks to them, he'd be giving the shoes away tonight. Screw them.

Andre pulled the brim of his knit hat down on his head and crossed over to the park. Nothing to it. He walked right up to where the large homeless man was sleeping on a large piece of cardboard, covered up in a smelly sleeping bag, color undeterminable in the dark. For the first time, Andre noticed another person sleeping just a few feet away. Another guy, he thought. This other guy wore a black hat pulled all the way over his face. He was curled up on his side with about four jackets on, knees pulled up to his chest. An old filthy blanket was draped across his legs. Dang, this dude was sleeping right on top of the grass.

The stench was pretty powerful, but Andre didn't care. He'd only be there for a second. No wonder he could hear the snoring from across the street, both guys were sawing some serious logs.

Andre tiptoed up to the guy in the sleeping bag and, without making a sound, dropped the new pair of Nikes on top of the collection of bags, water jugs, newspapers, whatever, all the crap that lay next to his sleeping hulk.

Big dude. Andre came to the same conclusion a few other times, having seen the guy in this park just about every time of day or night he passed by over the last two weeks. By his reckoning, the size 11s ought to fit the dude. Andre gave the shoes one last glance then took off for home. Damn things should be his.

§ § §

The next day after school Andre hurried home to get there before his dad did. He'd get an earful if the stupid garbage cans weren't out on the curb like they're supposed to be. That, of course, would lead to the laundry not being folded like they'd told him to which, in turn, would become a full-out scream scene about Andre's room, Andre's bathroom, and Andre's homework. Bleah, bleah, bleah! What a life he had!

What a stupid, miserable, ridiculous life. If only his parents would take a minute to just understand him. Look at things from his point of view. Listen and have a little patience without always TELLING him things. Every day, every night, same old crap. The only way to escape it was to escape it all. Get out and stay away for as long as he could, as soon as he could. Yes, as soon as Andre could work it out he'd show them.

Oops, there's the guy in the park, sitting with his buddy on the bench, wearing the new shoes!

Andre knew being homeless was not a good situation to be in, but come on. It couldn't be all that bad. Look at this dude, in his new Nikes just hanging out in the park. Laughing with his friend and doggin' anything and everything. Not taking any disrespect crap from anybody. Probably been out there all day long. Man, it just couldn't be all that bad. No hassles, absolutely none of the crap.

As Andre walked closer he could see the guy's new shoes were untied. In fact, what do you know, he could hear him talking about those shoes now.

"Outta nowhere, man, the shoes were just there this morning! Shit, I musta picked them up somewhere, right? And just forgot about them or something, that's all. These are my cool rocks, man. I'm stylin' now, you know it." He took a long drink from a bottle wrapped up tightly in a brown paper bag.

"Yeah, cool shoes is right, big man." His friend reached for the bottle and, after a moment's hesitation, the big dude reluctantly shared with him. He snatched back the bag as soon as the guy finished taking a little swig.

"Oh yeah, gotta go back and play me some hoops in these bad

boys. Y'know what I'm sayin? Two-handed dunk on these muthas, you know. Swish, swish." He savored one last drink and threw the bottle at the nearest trashcan. Missed.

Andre heard the bottle break in the bag.

Dang it, it was time to get home.

He smiled, knowing he'd be back later.

§§§

Later that night, Andre snuck out of the house again and walked back to the park, a shadow among shadows. Ah, but he carried another gift for his homeless friend. One new pair of shoes—good luck. Another brand new pair of shoes—GREAT luck!

And that's what Andre had, another pair of brand new Adidas he swiped from the locker room in the gym at school. Screw that, damn rich high school punk wasn't gonna miss these anyway. His rich folks would take him out for another pair. Shit, he probably already had another pair at home! Couldn't live with just one pair of cool shoes, right? One for school, one for play, hell, one or two more for everything else.

Andre cruised up to the sleeping homeless man and saw the blue Nikes peeking out from under his ratty sleeping bag. Andre may have been imagining, but it looked like the guy had a little smile on his face. See? New shoes will do that for you. Screw his parents. Well, the dude's smile ought to be big and bright when he woke up tomorrow and found another pair of brand spanking new shoes waiting for him.

He quietly left the new pair of Adidas beside the man's stash pile, covering them up a little bit with some old shirt. No sense in leaving them out in the open for someone else to snatch before dude woke up.

§§§

The next day after school Andre returned to the park and the scene of his... what, not a crime! Hell, he was giving the homeless guy a gift, not breaking any laws or anything. Well, maybe when he stole the shoes from school, but, dammit, he was right. The kid had on another pair of $150 shoes that same freakin' morning! B.F.D., Andre was just doing a good deed. Like Robin Hood, steal from the rich and give to the homeless, that's all. Hell, he wasn't even keeping the damn shoes for HIMSELF. That's what he SHOULD be doing!

There was the dude now, hanging out at the same park bench with his homeless friend. Oh wait a minute. The dude had on the Nikes, but his friend was wearing the Adidas! Hold on, that's not what Andre wanted to happen. Now what?

Andre came up closer to them, not sure what he was going to do. The dang Adidas were even too big for that other guy. He had on like four pairs of socks and some newspaper or rags stuffed into the shoes to keep them on. Andre could see it all peeking out over the top of the heel. What the hell?!

"Man," the guy wearing the Adidas was telling the big guy. "Thanks for these new shoes, man, thanks for these shoes. I can't believe your luck man. You are one righteous dude, too, to sell me these! Damn, these are really great shoes. Best shoes I ever had."

"Hey, we friends, right? It's cool. You paid a fair price for them so that's good for me, too."

The big guy took a drink from a much larger bottle wrapped in a brown paper bag. He took a long drink and smacked his lips smugly, wiping them dry with a big, meaty fist. "Man, this is good shit! And even after buying this drink I still got me a few bucks left. Party tonight!"

"That's right. Fair price for these bad boys. And I don't even want any of your drink 'cause you gave me a fair price for these shoes. Unless of course you want to share, well then that's okay 'cause we buds and all, you know."

The bottle was not offered, but no offense was taken.

Okay, Andre thought, okay. Well, dude sold the Adidas to his friend. That's cool, I guess. Now he gets to party, so he's happy. Plus, the other dude is happy, too, so whatever. Everyone's happy, everyone's got new shoes. F-that, every one's happy except Andre. He went on home.

§§§

That night, Andre crept into his parents' bedroom. He slowly opened their closet door. Not a sound. Good. Stepping into the closet, Andre reached around toward the back wall towards his dad's shoe rack. They were there somewhere, somewhere, yes! Got 'em! Andre silently closed the closet door and eased back out of the room.

Cool, he had his dad's new shoes, some freakin' I-talian real leather shoes! For work, his dad had said when Andre complained about not getting the new shoes he wanted. How much were these shoes, Dad, two hundred bucks? Two-fifty? That wasn't right. No sir, not fair at all. It wasn't like Andre was a total screw up. He did his school work, his chores for the most part. Yeah, he forgot sometimes, but no big deal really. He didn't even have a cell phone or iPad, no TV in his room—most of the people he knew did. Stayed away from gangs, too. Hell, he was his own gang. The Robin Hood Homeless Shoe Gang. Big freakin' deal. Screw it.

He took the shoes down to the park, strolling casually between the street and the trees, out of sight. Yeah, this was his time. He felt good out here.

The same two guys were camped out in the same spot again. Wow, they hadn't been rousted out by cops or anything.

They were asleep again, both wearing their new shoes and snoring as loud as hell. This time they had stupid, shitty grins on their faces. Andre noticed there were a number of empty bottles strewn about where they lay. There were some 40-ouncers, other smaller bottles, and plenty of different labels. Damn, looked like they had some party going on tonight. Good, let them. He was glad to bring them some happiness.

Seeing them in a drunken stupor, Andre felt bolder and walked right up to the big dude. He took his dad's leather shoes and placed them snugly in the arms of the sleeping guy. The guy took a hold of them, still asleep. Damn, dude was rank. Andre went home.

§§§

That next afternoon at the park, Andre was surprised to see a real party going on. Four other guys were hanging out on the bench with the big guy and his buddy, drinking from beer and whiskey bottles and passing around a glass pipe that was refilled and re-lit every now and again. A small, battery-powered boom box played some old time hip-hop music. Homeless Big Dude was wearing his Nikes, but Andre noticed that his friend did not have on the Adidas. He had on some old raggedy pair of boots.

One of the others brought a little plastic bag from his coat pocket. He dropped something from it into the pipe bowl. A lighter flared up and the guy took a deep drag from the pipe before passing it on for the next toke. The party wasn't very loud, but man they were all pretty wasted. Just right out in the park, out in the open.

At first, Andre thought they were having a discussion of some sort, like people usually do at parties, but they weren't. They were talking all right, but mostly they were talking to themselves. Addressing ghosts or shadows only they could see. Mostly muttering bizarre, drugged up gibberish into thin air.

Big Dude was calling out to someone, but Andre could hardly understand him. Andre leaned forward and strained to hear what the guy was saying and, when he caught the guy's voice for a minute, Andre smiled. Homeless dude was trying to send praise to his "Shoe God", Andre heard him say, for giving him all of those new shoes.

Andre snickered as he continued to spy on them from behind a tree. Great. Shoe God. Damn Shoe God got them all messed up!

Then he realized HE was the damn Shoe God. Andre. Yup. And he had another pair to drop off that night. Hopefully things would be quiet by then. Yeah, some shoes he ripped off a punk freshman right after the dude had been showing them off to his buds. That's what you get for spending so much money and then showing them off like some valuable treasure. Gone, taken by the bad-ass Shoe God! He shifted his backpack and then the Shoe God left them all to their party so he could get something to eat at home.

§ § §

51

That night Andre could tell right off things weren't right at the park. From two blocks away, he saw flashing lights coming from that direction, reflecting off the low rain clouds and mist that had rolled in that evening. He tried to be even more discreet than usual as he edged nearer to the park entrance.

Dang, there were three cop cars parked right inside the park, next to that same park bench. Two of the cop cars had their lights flashing. Andre could also see there were two other unmarked cars as well. Dark sedans—obviously police, detectives, or something. A number of officers in rain gear stood off to the side of a cordoned off area near some bushes. Yellow police tape kept them back like a force field while two men in dark coveralls were inside the tape. Both held clipboards and one of them was on a cell phone.

Oh crap, Andre realized, they're looking at some body splayed out on the ground. Hell, that's where big dude and his friend had been sleeping. Nah, couldn't be. Could it? There was a blanket or something covering the body so he couldn't tell from where he was standing.

But then he saw it: one foot wasn't covered all the way and that foot was wearing a brand-new freakin' Nike AirMax, black with the royal blue heel. Andre shifted the pack on his back, the heel from one of the stolen shoes digging into his back. Damn, big dude bought it. Was he murdered, OD or something? Man, how did he die?

Andre couldn't help it. He drew closer to the whole scene, knowing he somehow played some part in it, made a connection, even if that connection was just the dang shoes. He stepped out of the shadows and tried to get a closer look. Andre came up to the low iron fence near the bushes and the taped-off area, trying to see what was going on. The pulsating police lights were blinding every time they flashed. Did they really need these on? Andre could hardly see what the two men were doing, writing on their clipboards, talking on the cell phone still.

"Hey, you, step back please." One of the other policemen had seen him and left the group. He approached Andre. "What are you doing out here?"

"Just saw the lights and wanted to check it out," Andre replied.

"Well, this is a crime scene so you shouldn't be here." The officer looked at Andre with a critical eye. "You know this person? Name is...was Adamaceo Cleveland—went by Big Maceo."

"Nah, just seen him hanging around out here all the time. Him and his homeless homeys, just bs'ing, drinking, you know. Hanging."

"Yeah, well this guy's not hanging out anywhere anymore, except maybe the morgue."

Andre flinched a little at the thought. "So what happened to him?"

"Don't know really. Far as we can tell so far, this guy had been partying pretty hard with his friends all day. He passed out right there, and his friends just left. Died sometime later. Probably OD."

"Man, that's crappy."

"Yeah, it happens too often. Some of them would rather party than eat. They get a little cash and there's only one thing on their mind, you know? And look at those shoes, man, he's got better shoes on that I have."

"Yeah," Andre murmured softly. "Me too."

"Well, according to one of his buddies, this guy came into some pretty good cash. Spent it on a load of booze and crack and they all went at it hard. They said he sold some shoes he found, got paid a pretty good price for some leather ones. Nobody knew where he got those killer shoes. The Shoe Fairy, I guess. Killer shoes, that's a good one, yeah?"

Nah, Andre thought to himself, those killer shoes came directly from the Shoe God.

"Anyway," the cop went on. "Guess he got a good enough price to throw one last party. Good enough to have a party to last the rest of his life. Now you've got to leave this area, unless you have any info for us."

Suddenly, the stolen pair of shoes Andre was carrying in his backpack weighed a ton. Without answering the officer, Andre turned and walked away, back across the street from the park, back into the shadows he preferred.

When Andre was further down the street and sure he was out of any policeman's view, he stopped. He took the shoes out of his back-pack. He tied the laces together in a knot, then stood and looked up.

With one motion Andre heaved the shoes up to the nearest power line, where they deftly hooked over the wire. The shoes swung crazily for a moment, and then, like the quiet of the still night, came to rest. The Shoe God was officially out of business.

BUS PASS

Based on the fable "The Old Woman and the Wine Bottle": A very old woman out for her daily walk finds an empty wine jug on the trail near her cottage. At first angry at the thoughtlessness of someone leaving garbage lying about, she stoops carefully to pick up the jug and catches the slight fragrance of the rich grapes once contained therein. The smell causes her to reminisce about her days of youth, of fine wine, of romance.

The moral of the fable is: What memories cling 'round the instruments of our pleasure.

It was a sunny day, sunny but windy.

On the day they buried Jenny it had been pretty much the same type of day, but so much hotter. Or perhaps only he felt the heat that day. His shirt was thoroughly drenched with perspiration after the short ceremony. When he finally took off his jacket that night, he just stuffed the shirt into the trash.

Valentine's Day. Crap. The second Valentine's Day in a row he had come for a visit to the cemetery. He had a dozen red roses for her that first time, her favorite flower. This time he'd brought two dozen. And the next time he would bring three dozen, then four, until he had to cart them up here by the box load.

He looked past her headstone, out beyond the thick wrought-iron fence, past the scattered evergreen trees. The bay, far below in the distance, glistened in the bright sunlight, dotted with millions of small whitecaps stirred up by the breeze. The sailboats out on the bay were so far away that it was difficult to discern their movement. It was as if they were just tiny little pictures of sailboats pasted here and there on blue paper. But if he stared at one long enough, it finally did move just a bit. He took a long, deep breath, just beginning to feel relaxed again.

The morning had been thrown off by some freaky bag lady. It surprised him she upset him so much, but he assumed he was just overly tense from planning his trip out to visit Jenny. He had taken the day off from work to spend time here. Of course his boss had given him hell again, but, well, it was his earned vacation time, so what could Mr. Fitzgerald do? Nothing, that's what. And he would complete the cursed Braggs Project soon enough, anyhow. An extra day wouldn't matter, they were already ten days late with the proposal now. Besides, Clayton Braggs was a widower himself. If he had to, he could and WOULD explain the situation. He was pretty sure Braggs would understand.

That morning he'd gone to have a cappuccino and Danish pastry at The Coffee Shop, a place Jenny and he spent many a Sunday morning. Today he sat himself at an outdoor table in the morning sun. They had often sat there together in the same exact spot, talking, laughing, silent. Memories of their life together, pictured as clearly as if they had happened just moments earlier, ran easily through his mind. But it was over two years now. Two years. The memories were still clear. That is, they were clear until some ruckus behind him disrupted his reverie.

Gawd, it was some old, dingy bag lady. She must have begged the owner enough to get a free cup of coffee. There she sat, having a perfectly absurd conversation with herself, talking loudly enough for everybody to hear. Using only his peripheral vision, he watched her first stick a grimy finger into her mouth. Then the woman dipped it into a packet of Sweet 'N Lo, using the same finger to stir and sweeten her coffee at the same time. The only time her chattering stopped was when she popped her dripping finger into her mouth and slurped. Even that she did noisily. He wondered if it was that sound or her prattling, but something about her made him feel slightly nauseous when he glanced her way.

She sat a table away, her four green garbage bags piled next to her. Each no doubt stuffed full of her life's treasures, intertwined and knotted together with a brown bath towel. One leg, red, puffy, and raw-looking, was draped over them for protection. Protection from what, only she knew. He couldn't tell what the original color of her dirty, untied hiking boot was, but it certainly didn't match the other Converse shoe she wore on the other foot. Except, that is, in greasy filth.

"I had fifty of them one time, 1972 or '73," she was saying, slowly finger-stirring-sweetening her coffee. "Yeah now, oh yes, we were, that was, a true, true indication, you know."

She stopped to suckle. It reminded him of a big, ugly, dirty pig sucking on its mother-pig's ugly, dirty teat, drooling and making grunting sounds.

He couldn't help noticing other café patrons rolling their eyes and shaking their heads with pity. Most turned away and pretended she wasn't there. A couple nearby got up and took their food and drink back inside the café. He also saw the lady was not aware of any of this. She just sat, drinking her coffee, dunking her fingers, guarding her stuff, and talking.

"No, no, NO!" she said a bit louder. "That's just NOT IT, not it at all! It's been discussed many, many times! What's the reason? Hmmm, that was a nice time out there!"

He chanced a longer glance at her just as she turned her face towards him and their eyes met. Then she did something that immediately gave him that nauseous feeling again. She pointed her wet, dirty finger right at him. But he spun away quickly, his downcast eyes finding a catch-spot on the gold wedding band he still wore.

"Oh, okay, staring now, is it, staring? Yeah, they look, sure, look away, look all they want. Look at Mrs. Kreiberg! Go AHEAD!"

He was sure she was speaking to him, but he was too embarrassed to look again. She, on the other hand, was not too embarrassed to continue.

"Don't even think it, even think it. Zooooom! Wow-Look! Isn't it just great that life meets life, and coffee starts the day, but coffee is a true, true—oh, HELL, awwww, no!"

There was a loud splatter and it was her cup rolling across the table. Chair legs scraped backwards suddenly and he knew without looking she managed to knock over her cup of coffee.

"Aw, blast this old hand and cup, old woman, can't even trust a good eating establishment anymore without..."

He braved one more glance and saw her scraping the spilled coffee off the table edge with one hand, back into her coffee cup held in the other.

It was his turn to shake his head.

A young woman called a waitress over, said something and pointed in the bag lady's direction. He waited to see if the waitress would approach her, but she didn't. He glanced inside the café once or twice and wondered why nobody came out to escort the street woman away quietly.

He didn't feel like finishing his pastry or coffee, so he brushed his mouth with his napkin, dropped it over his garbage, and left. As he exited, he imagined the old lady grabbing his leftovers and stuffing them into her mouth, but he forgot all about her by the time he drove away and headed towards the cemetery. He soon arrived, parked and made his slow way to Jenny's gravesite.

Still clutching the roses, he took a deep breath and rolled his head to loosen his neck and shoulder muscles. He pulled a couple of folded paper towels from his pants pocket and brushed some dirt off of Jenny's marble headstone. Over the last two years it had become more and more dirty, not as polished and shiny as it once was.

He sat down on the grass, crossing his legs and leaning a shoulder against the marble stone. Being out here next to Jenny always felt so good. It felt comforting, yet he couldn't figure out why he didn't visit more often.

The roses he brought wouldn't fit in the small, partially buried metal cup used for that purpose, so, making a mental note to bring a vase with him the next time out, he laid the flowers gently against the headstone. Pretty.

Suddenly, wild laughter split the peaceful air and he jumped to his feet, startled at first, then angry. His heart was pounding.

"What the hell?" he said aloud, looking left, then right. "Oh, my gawd."

It was her! It was that same old bag lady. There she was at a gravesite not thirty feet away! And she was laughing loudly and talking, still talking.

"Ha, ha, ha, aha, ha! That was a good one, no, Mr. Kreiberg, ha, ha, aha, aha, heh, heh-heh, heh, a GREAT one, it was, ha, ha-ha-heh!! You know, that reminds me."

He couldn't believe it! Running his hands through his hair in frustration, he closed his eyes and took a deep breath. What the hell was going on here? His eyes re-opened but she was still there.

He squinted at her to get a better look. Yes, damn it, it was her again! And what was she doing? Cleaning a headstone? Yes, kneeling there in her ripped, green and beige dress, red sweater, and non-matching shoes, surrounded by all sorts of cleaning paraphernalia!

She sprayed a corner of the stone with a can of something that foamed up quickly. Then she spritzed it with a spray bottle. Picking up a stiff cleaning brush, she scrubbed hard at the area, again and again, back and forth. Pulling a dirty rag out from under one knee, she then wiped at the spot, sprayed yet another can of something else over it and wiped at it even more. Examining the now spotless eight inch square area of white marble diligently with one eye closed, she finally spit on the stone. This seemed to be some sign of approval for the work she had done. She made one last graceful swipe with her rag, and then started the whole process all over again at another spot. And all the while she carried on some sort of wild, sing-song, conversational monologue, since there was no one else around talking with her.

He sat down again, leaning his back against Jenny's gravestone, facing the wild lady. All of a sudden, he was beside himself, suddenly bone weary yet strangely fascinated watching the woman clean the entire stone chattering and carrying on. She was full of movement and a weird sense of elegance.

"Now, Henry, my Henry, hasn't it? I know I haven't been able to get back lately, but I've been busy, you know, running around. You know the peace talks are off again."

She emptied one of her cans and, after one final attempt to spray with nothing shooting forth, reached into her assortment of bags to pull out another one. She banged it against the headstone once and sprayed it on.

"Gladys and Barry Winger moved back to Idaho last week. Their son must've called for them, you think? Son of a sunova, sunuv, ooh that Gladys, what a freak! A freak! Did you know that a bunch of kids went to Africa and spoke at the Mandela Foundation about peace? I gave Gladys a present when they shipped out. A piece of chain I had, bright chain, or was it a lid to a bowl? I'm not sure now."

The woman paused her monologue to wipe her brow. With a quick blow of her nose on a filthy rag followed by a swipe to brush the hair from her eyes, she prattled on.

"Hey, gotta finish here, Mr. Kreiberg, you know, the bus, oh yeah, yes. The bus keeps rolling along. Hey—we got pictures of Mars! I've got my sun place to go to every day over cross-town now. Lord, it's been beautiful lately! Yeah, you're home, you're at home, my Henry, so don't give me none of your, those ideas, okay? In case you don't know, the Saints won the Bowl. Yep. And another condor was born. You probably know."

By then, she finished the entire headstone and it literally sparkled in the sunlight. Still kneeling, the woman gathered all of her things and dropped them slowly, one at a time, into her bags. She knotted them again and stood somewhat painfully, stretching and arching her back. She happened to glance his way. Like super-strong magnets their eyes locked for the second time that day.

"Still staring, man? Still just looking? Didn't you hear what I said?" She yelled to him, draping the bags over her shoulders. "Did you hear what I told you?"

He didn't turn from her this time. Alone together in the cemetery, he felt compelled to call out to her. "What? What do you want? What are you saying?"

She placed one filthy hand on Henry Kreiberg's gravestone. "The Dead. Home. You know it. The Dead go home. Like my husband, my Henry, he went early. I'm just trying to make things as interesting as possible until my bus pass expires. You should try that. Quit watching.

What do you do if you're dead but ain't dead? Same thing if you're living but ain't living, right? It's as simple as that, you know?"

She turned to leave.

And as she did her words echoed in his mind, "… same thing if you're living but ain't living, right?" Right?

And in that brief moment, in an instant of pure clarity, that crazy old bag lady made perfect sense. He understood exactly what she was trying to explain to him, his mind flashing on everything he had done since Jenny's passing. Really though, it was everything he had NOT done, all he easily excused himself from. All of the living he put on hold. What a waste of time.

Jenny would not have been happy with him.

He realized in that split second the old bag lady just taught him a very good lesson, a life-saving one. It was just enough and just in time.

"Wait," he called, standing. He scooped up the roses, first dropping a couple into the empty cup by Jenny's headstone.

"Here," he said, walking over to her. "These flowers—they're for you."

She took the bunch into her grimy hands, set them down lightly atop her bags, and ambled away.

"You don't want to miss your bus," he said to her back.

"You do the same," she replied, walking straight away.

He didn't make it back to the cemetery for some time, long after the Braggs Project was done. But when he did make it back, he found a bright, red rose in the flower cup at Jenny's grave. And Jenny's headstone was so clean it sparkled in the sun.

ONCE A HERO

Based on the fable "The Jay and the Peacock": The peacock spread his glorious tail feathers, showing off the colors of the rainbow for all gathered to see, and mocked a nearby jay for the drab colors of its boring plumage. The jay only laughed and scolded the peacock, reminding him that while he himself soared about the heavens singing for the world to hear, the peacock could only walk on the ground, as a chicken among the dunghills.

Moral: It is not only fine feathers that make the bird.

When I was eight years old, he was my hero.

Travis Waller was only four years older than me, but that was a lifetime. He was bigger than life. I would watch him out there, running as fast as he could, sprinting in the open court, hustling back on defense. The guy would just stick people, make the perfect bounce pass, grind out the extra two yards, and always go first to third on the slow liner in the hole. He never did run the fastest, jump the highest, and wasn't very big. Travis was kind of wiry.

But Travis Waller had what my fifth grade teacher called "grit". My eighth grade government teacher called it "heart". And he displayed what both the varsity basketball coach and the varsity football coach called "guts". But when I was a kid growing up, I thought Travis Waller was "the best". Travis never gave up. The guy was tireless. Whatever the contest, he never quit. It must have been a nightmare to play against him, a relentless, determined, maniacal nightmare. Always there. Always struggling. Seemingly always in control.

The neighborhood park director would take us younger kids to the junior high to watch the school team play. No matter what the sport, Travis was out there. I think he was the captain of every team he joined.

It seemed like it, anyway. And if he wasn't, then Travis sure led by sheer will and example.

When I grew older, I got to watch him in high school. Travis did it all. There he moved beyond the boundaries of normal sports. How he casually excelled in all areas! Travis dated the head football cheerleader, of course. He was voted Homecoming King, which I didn't think was anything to brag about at the time, until I saw that the Queen was Meredith Bradley. Christ Almighty! Travis even had a part in the school play, not the lead, mind you, but a pretty big part. It was as if Travis was the "name" and folks came out to see him as much as or more than the rest of the group, whatever was going on. Travis Waller made every activity an event.

When I was a freshman at Galveon High School, Travis Waller was a senior. I made the junior varsity team, pretty good for only a freshman. At track practice after school, I completed a 440 yard practice run and was completing my slow, cool-down walk along the perimeter of the track, daydreaming about the Olympic gold medal I had just won. The sun just started to drop in the sky when there he was, shouting at me across the way, "Hey! Pretty good run, Hampton!"

Travis Waller didn't have to say it. Travis Waller chose to say it. It took me a moment to realize he even knew my name—hell, last name anyway! But, hey, why wouldn't he know me? We hung out at the same playground for most of our lives. It didn't matter his group of friends rarely bothered with the "little guys". We lived in the same neighborhood, read the same daily sports page from the same hometown newspaper. Even went to the same corner store for sodas and chips after ballgames. I stopped, tres-casually, of course, to say "Thanks," but he already walked away. Nevertheless, that just about made my whole week. I still remember it so fondly now.

Then I guess what usually happens, happened. As I got older and into my own little post-but-not-post-enough-pubescent/adult world, I lost track of him. I mean, it wasn't like I stalked the guy or was in love with him or anything. He had just been an ever-present part of my growing up. A part that always seemed a bit out of my grasp, yet always noticeable. Comfortable, you know? Right there if I ever really looked. It's surprising to me when I look back, I realize how easy it was to simply allow this part of my youth to quietly dissolve away. Sort of like an old finger wart—for a while it's always around. Eventually you notice it only some of the time. Then it starts getting better until finally it's completely gone. By that time, you've already pretty much forgotten it was ever there.

Except the truth was I never really forgot about him, there or not. Travis Waller was my sports hero—my childhood idol. Of course I didn't call him that when we were growing up. Mostly I called him a stud. And growing up, I couldn't really allow myself to think too much about it. But sometimes, when I didn't think I could run another step or the bases were loaded and the count was full in the bottom of the eighth or I had to call Nancy McDavid to ask her to the Junior Prom, I remembered Travis. It was all about grit, heart, guts.

My wonder of him wouldn't let me quit, wouldn't let me give up. You know, that "What would Travis Waller think of me?" kind of thing. I believed that if he was in the exact same situation, he wouldn't quit. Knowing that made me not want to give up either. I would picture him in my mind, grit my teeth tighter, set my jaw, and just give it a go.

I heard bits of news about him from time to time. Just casual talk, usually. Once in a while a reference about him in the town paper. Like the time he ran for 234 yards and three touchdowns against Jackson Community College when he was a sophomore at that small junior college up north. Or when some guy named Morris lettered in three sports as a junior. He was the first athlete to earn that many since the legendary Travis Waller earned four in three straight years. I heard Travis moved up to some four-year school in Oregon to play football and run track. A good time later, I heard he had done well in football, but wasn't fast enough for the track team. But I remember reading he was good enough to be a second string running back and a starting defensive back at that Oregon school. Once he had two interceptions, one for a touchdown in some game against a rival state college. But other than that, news about him and his exploits sort of dried up. Or maybe I started paying less attention.

After a while I heard Travis Waller hadn't finished college. He'd blown out a knee or something. Hadn't made it back home, either, as far as I knew. In fact, I heard more times than I wanted to that Travis had gotten into partying and grass and coke and who knows what else. No one ever spoke too much about it. Just tidbits of information to make you feel like you had the inside story — a little gossip to make you feel some small town excitement. I never paid too much attention to the talk or attempted to find out more about the situation either way.

I got better in high school. I found out I could be a slightly-better-than-average athlete, if I prepared myself mentally and physically, and tried to keep one step ahead of my competition. But that was a problem — when you're muddling through high school a lot of other crap gets in your way. Classes, peer pressure (a term you only understand later in life), girls, money, acne, beer and pot, and, and, and. The list goes on forever. Plus, it was hard to be prepared while you were trying to look like you weren't trying too hard to prepare and fit in. So I did okay, but doing okay took up a lot of my time. I guess I enjoyed it. Just wanted to be a decent human being.

Went away to college, and, unlike Travis Waller, I returned home after graduating with a degree in accounting. I started out in biology, but numbers seemed a safer, more logical science. Learning biology was like learning a new language. Why study the Latin name for animal species and sub-families? The Latin names usually meant something like "big, furry head with large teeth" or "walks in mud and climbs upside down" or "eyes rotate like pepperoni pizza" anyway. Why not just learn those terms? Now those names I could remember. I just didn't have the time or patience for all that other stuff.

I ended up working for a real estate office right in town, analyzing financial statements, taxes, loan applications, that kind of thing. Everything was aimed at searching for and mortgaging the American dream. It wasn't too bad and I got to see and visit with a lot of the folks from town.

Can't even begin to describe how much I missed home while I was away to school. I'm almost embarrassed to think about it. It affected my college work, but who cares? All you needed were C's and D's to get your degree. When I returned home, I packed up my degree in a box with some other old junk and squirreled it away in the attic or garage or some place. To be honest, I'm not really sure where.

One night, a couple of years after entering the work force, I met up with a college friend at a real estate seminar. We went out for drinks and a snack afterwards. Who would have guessed his date would call me a week later to ask if I would accompany her to some two-act community play in town?

That was all it took, followed shortly by a downhill slide all the way to marriage. A home, two cars, too much debt, a daughter, using up any savings we had accumulated separately or together, complaining about taxes, another child, a boy, two years later. Now I've been married nine years. My daughter Jane turned eight. My boy, Scott, is six. She likes school, he doesn't. She changes attitudes daily, he does every fifteen minutes. My wife, Marilyn, works as a County administrator. She's kind of a big-wig, but we both wish she could go part-time. We try to share taking care of the kids after school but Marilyn gets awful busy sometimes. We do the school volunteer thing together. Personally, between you and me, the best part about my job now as a real estate broker is I can call my office at 8:57 in the morning from beneath my bed sheets and say, without any guilt at all, "I have a meeting with a client at 9:30, so I won't be in until after lunch." Hey, it pays the bills, you know? Plus, people get truly happy when they buy a home, almost every time.

Sometimes I just get this urge to do something. What should I call it, charitable? Maybe. Something to benefit my brethren mankind, or womankind. My attempts to be charitable hold no sexual bias. You know, it always seems to happen around that holiday time of the year, Thanksgiving—"Let us give thanks for all that we have, bless those less fortunate," and Christmas—"Peace on Earth, Goodwill to Man/Woman/Child!" That kind of thing.

Sometimes I think my goodwill to mankind is a by-product of all the Hallmark Greeting Card commercials I've seen on television. But hey, that's just another good New Year's Eve bar discussion.

This brings me, on this Thanksgiving morning, to the Stoddard

Community Recreation Hall located in the town just west of thriving Galveon, my hometown. I did some serious thinking about volunteering to help serve turkey dinners to those of our community who were less fortunate. Marilyn and I both believed this was a great idea and there really wasn't anything pressing at home. I promised to be home in time to help finish cooking the turkey dinner, start a fire in the fireplace, and make the hors d'oeuvres. Besides, my daughter Jane loves this. She just couldn't wait to help serve. At her school, they constantly talk about helping our less fortunate neighbors: sharing, volunteering, Earth Day, things like that. And maybe I was just ever-slightly motivated because it could be a good way to network with people from the community. You know, generate new contacts for the business and all.

I watch Jane help to put placemats and plastic knives and forks out on all of the folding tables. She's got her nametag and everything: "Jane—Volunteer". The other women volunteers, in whose charge she has fallen, all take special turns to say to me as I meander by, "Your daughter is just great!", and "Janie is such a special kid!" ("It's JANE!" Jane replies in turn, a twinkle in her charitable eyes), and, of course, "You're such a lucky father!"

I know, I nod. I know.

The problem is that's all I've been doing for the last forty-five minutes—looking busy. The truth was I wasn't busy at all. I guess a whole lot of other people feel like helping out this time of year, too. We must have watched the same holiday greeting card commercials or something.

It was a piece of cake signing in and getting my nametag filled out. Here it was, right on my shirt pocket: Daniel. Me. Not DANIEL—VOLUNTEER, but that's okay, everyone here should know. And placed on just right ("Jane is such a special child" always puts those nametags on straight!). After signing in I was pointed in the direction of the kitchen, my chosen area of assistance.

Jane just got swooped right up.

"Margaret, we need someone to help with the utensils!"

"Jane, dear, you can do that, can't you? Judy, here's someone to do that!"

Time for just one last, "Daddy, when are we going to help with the dinners?", then off she went, holding the hand of a volunteer dressed up in her best pilgrim shift, gold-buckled shoes and bonnet.

"So, that way to the kitchen, right?" I asked the lady at the front desk.

"Right," she replied. She squinted at my nametag. "Ugh, Daniel, do you know Fred Parkerson? He's in charge of the kitchen? No? Well, he's wearing the brown and orange apron with the turkey on the front. Go on and see him. He'll get you busy."

Of course, once in the kitchen nobody knew where Fred was located. Probably off setting up the juice area or getting the last of the cooked birds cut and packed in the warming trays. Some old guy suggested I wait right there for Fred, he should be along any minute. Also, could I please move back a little bit since I was blocking the potato mashers? The boiled potatoes would be done in a few minutes. I did, and there I stood shuffling from foot to foot, just waiting for Fred.

You know, you just can't imagine the amount of activity going on around you when you have absolutely nothing to do. You're positively almost-in-pain-ready to do anything for anyone, in need or not, just so you're doing SOMETHING. I was here to volunteer, for chrissakes!

So I did. And nobody was safe.

"Here, let me help you with that carton of milk. Where would you like it? Oh, you didn't need it moved? Sorry."

"Does anyone know where Fred is?"

"Oh, here, let me help you with. Ooooh. Ouch. Wow, I'm sorry, didn't mean to do that."

"Where should these trays go? They're okay right here, all right then, right here they shall stay."

"Fred? Are you Fred Parkinson? What's that? Oh, yeah, Parkerson. Yeah, oh, you're not?"

"Careful with that knife there, sir. Here, let me show you how to hold—Oh, right, okay, you got it, sorry about that, didn't mean to scare you."

"Doesn't anyone know where Fred is?"

"There must be some dishes to wash or towels to wring out or something."

"Hey, WHERE THE HECK IS FRED?!"

A man in a bright orange apron with a big red turkey made out of glued-on rhinestones touched me on the sleeve.

"Hi, I'm Fred. What can I do for you?"

Relieved, I gushed, "Fred, Fred, finally. I'm Daniel, I'm a volunteer!" At last.

"For the kitchen?!" Fred squealed this—yes, squealed. "Danny, we're just about all done here. God, where were you two hours ago when I could have used you?"

I assume Fred Parkerson understood the sinking of my heart from the look of total humiliation in my eyes.

"Now, wait, Danny-boy, I actually think Sammie could use a little help in the walk-in there. Come with me."

Good ol' Fred.

He led me into a huge walk-in freezer. The giant door was propped open by a monster-sized, deformed pumpkin. On a counter along one side there was a short table with silver, oval serving trays full of one-inch square pats of butter, each on its own piece of one and one-half inch cardboard square. An older woman was there, placing six pats of butter each onto small paper plates. She moved the plates onto a tray already stacked full of plates of butter pats, then grabbed another empty paper plate. Pats of butter everywhere.

"Sammie, you've been in this cold storage long enough. This is Daniel, he's come to help. Let's let him finish with the butter, okay?"

Sammie eyed me suspiciously for a moment, then handed me a small butter knife. Her nose had a bluish tinge on the tip. Her glasses were definitely a little foggy.

"Only six pats per plate, Daniel." She raised her eyebrows at me and walked out.

"Daniel, when you're finished here, put these trays on this cart, and then wheel this out to Bonnie on the food line. She's in charge of bread distribution." Fred patted me on the back. "Thanks for your help." He turned to go.

"What about serving?" I asked him. "My daughter and I will be helping with the food, right?"

"Got enough volunteers for that, Danny-o, and they're already at their stations. Most of the food's already out and ready to go. Butter's always last, you know, what with the melting and all. Thanks again!"

And out he went—out to his steaming trays of turkey and gravy, pots full of mashed potatoes and corn and peas. Food to be served to people who needed to be fed, by people who volunteered to help serve the food. People who knew to arrive a lot earlier than I did. Yeah, a lot earlier than Butter-Man Dandy Danny-o. I watched him go.

But, hey, that's okay. We all had to do our share of work to help benefit our brothers and sisters, right? With fervor strengthened by long minutes of intermittent wandering and standing around, I attacked my butter chore. Six pats to a plate, plenty of pats, plenty of plates. Pile them up in a tray then place the loaded trays on the cart. I can honestly say that I had never felt so good about the whole concept of butter as a necessary food group as I did just then, standing there in an ice-cold food locker, cutting up pats of butter and counting six and only six of those pats right out to be placed so swiftly onto those paper plates.

And I attack the all-important question: Should I stack the butter plates three high or four, maybe even five on those trays? Better stick with four, right between risky and perfectly safe. And when I completed my duty, what about the butter knife, my proud tool, nay, my FRIEND, constantly at my side in the execution of my duty? Well, I'll wash it AND dry it, of course, and place it ever so neatly right back on the counter top.

Okay. I was finished. My trays were all stacked on the cart, ready to wheel in to Bonnie, She Who Is In Charge of Bread Distribution.

I glanced at my watch before wheeling that butter-laden cart out to those hungry people—everyone wanted butter on their bread and potatoes, didn't they?! Well, that old butter chore took all of about ten minutes. Nine minutes and twenty-two seconds, actually.

But, hey, that's okay, I did my part. And now it was time to head out to the waiting masses.

"Make way for the butter cart!" I shouted as I wheeled the cart out of the walk-in.

I needn't have bothered. No one was left in the kitchen. I was all alone, just me and my appointed task. Rolling to the swinging doors leading out to the Hall, I spun in a tight circle and backed out the doors, so as not to run anyone down.

"Butter, coming throu—" I started to yell, but cut it short as all heads swiveled, all eyes turned to look at me. Yes, me, the idiotic person yelling out right in the middle of the benediction (a lovely prayer about brotherhood and sharing, of course!).

I dropped my eyes as I stopped in the middle of MY delivery. The things we volunteers have to deal with in pursuit of our chosen calling! As the prayer ended and "Amen" and "Hallelujah" filled the air I located the bread area and completed my duty.

"Bonnie," I bowed to the woman with the "Bonnie—Volunteer/ Food" name tag, with just a slight hint of satisfaction. "The butter has arrived." Have arrived? Oh, well.

Wiping my hands contentedly on my shirt, I scanned the now bustling and quickly filling room for Jane. The noise level began at a slow, but steady rise. There she was, still hard at work, helping a woman and two other children tie floating balloons to the center-pieces on each table. I went over to assist.

"Can I help?" I inquired.

Jane looked at me and raised her eyebrows. "Daddy! What were you doing making a commotion like that, and in the middle of grace! Are we still going to help feed the poor people?"

The woman, she must have been in charge of Balloon Decorations, came over.

"Hi, is this your Jane? You know, you truly are blessed, she is such a wonderful helper and just delightful! Janie, come here, I'll put up that last balloon and we'll be all done. Thanks so much for your help, and thank you, uh—Daniel, for letting us use Jane this morning. Such a delight, that child."

As I stood there, nodding and smiling, she ruffled Jane's hair and walked away, busily in search of the last balloon spot.

I took Jane's small hand and gave it a squeeze. She sighed.

"I'm tired, Daddy. I never knew volunteering was such hard work. You know, I haven't had a moment's rest since we got here! First I did the placemats, then the forks and stuff. Then we put all those flowers up, and the balloons. Oh, and a while ago I helped a lady named Jackie put a bunch of cans of stuff in small boxes with all of these other helpers. When we were all done the same priest that did that prayer said a prayer for US. He said he blessed all of us for our hard work and caring! Wasn't that great? Did you get blessed too, Daddy?"

I just stood there, smiling and nodding my head.

Finally, I shrugged and said, "Come on, Jane, let's go sit down for a sec. Sounds like you did a lot of hard work helping out. Let's go sit over there." I pointed to a spot by the stage where a small four-member group was getting set-up. They looked like country and western singers, their straw hats, bolo ties, and cowboy boots giving them away. I didn't really care since I didn't expect to be around much longer to find out.

"Shouldn't we be getting over to where the food is being passed out?"

"I don't think they need us to help with that today, Jane. Look, there are plenty of other helpers for that." I pointed to the row of food-serving volunteers, most of them with their food serving utensils at the ready, poised in front of steaming trays and awaiting the action.

"But I thought that's what we were going to do today, help to feed the homeless and poor?"

"Yeah, but you know, we helped out in a lot of others ways. Look at everything you did—you really helped a lot. Maybe next time we can help with the food part, too."

"Oh." She seemed sad, but, with her eight-year-old wisdom, got over it immediately. "Can I get something to drink, Dad? I'm really thirsty."

"I think so, honey, but let's sit first."

We made our way to a deserted table, turning to squeeze between folding chairs set close to each other. A big turnout was expected. We sat for a minute or two, taking in the holiday scene. Okay, I think that was enough sitting.

"You sit tight right here, Jane. I'll go get you a soda or something, okay?"

Jane sat down and I turned to go. As I did, a hand reached out and grasped mine, shaking gently. I noticed the man's eyes quickly scanning my nametag.

"Daniel. Hi, my name's Paul. How are you today? Here, have a seat here with your daughter. Your daughter, right? So how many will be in your party today?" He escorted me back down into my seat next to Jane.

"What's that? What?" I shook my head and faced Paul. "Hi. I'm Daniel. Uh-huh, this is my daughter, Jane."

"Pleased to meet you both. I'm so glad you could make it today." Paul seemed too happy. "So, how many will be with you today? Any other family, children, friends?"

"Oh, no, wait a minute, Paul," I replied. "We're not here to eat, we're volunteers." I pointed to my nametag. "See. DANIEL, that's me. I volunteered to help out in the kitchen serving food but I came too late. And, here, look at Jane's tag. See? JANE—VOLUNTEER. My daughter. She helped with balloons and stuff. No, we're not here to eat. We came to help."

Paul looked at me for a second, then at Jane's nametag. He smiled, just a tad sheepishly. "Oops, well thanks for helping out." He turned, immediately identifying "another" brother in need. He stepped away from us and held out his hand. "Hi, I'm Paul, how are you today?"

Jane took hold of my hand. "Gosh, Daddy, he thought we were homeless or something." She looked up at me, kind of half-smiling.

"Just another volunteer on a mission, dear," I answered, winking and flashing a big smile at her. "I'll go get your soda."

I walked over to the serving area or Food Distribution Center, as Fred would probably say, and located the beverages. Plastic boxes full of small milk cartons, tubs full of soda and ice, huge coffee pots and cups, stirring sticks, sugar and cream packets. I got in place at the end of the line that had already formed in front of Distribution Point A, or the table, as it is more commonly referred, about twenty deep. My attention focused on the activities directly in front of me. It had been a chilly morning and the coffee seemed like a hot ticket. Many others were grabbing cartons of milk as well. It does a body good, homeless or not, I guess. Sodas, naah, still kind of chilly out. Maybe later this afternoon. But our line was moving along, albeit rather slowly, as most of the coffee drinkers stopped for cream and sugar—hardly any takers for the Sweet 'N Lo.

It seemed like the Thanksgiving Dinner was going just great.

"Well, hello, Daniel, how are you?" A hand reached for mine again, a woman's this time.

"Hi," I muttered, shaking hands warily this time. "How are ya?"

"Just fine, sir." She smiled from beneath her white, starched pilgrim bonnet. "And how are you? Are you enjoying yourself today? Is there anything I can get for you? Do you have a place to sit? Is there any-one here with you today? Would you like me to introduce you to some of the other guests?"

I glanced at her nametag: Gloria.

"Well, Gloria," I started, "You are sure a welcome ray of light in my otherwise dreary life." But I couldn't keep it up. I didn't want to be cynical today. "No, seriously, I'm okay. I'm actually just getting a soda for my daughter. I'm a volunteer, not a guest."

Gloria smiled and shuffled away graciously.

Just then a man walked right up to the front of the drink line, just bypassed all of the other visitors and volunteers waiting patiently. He reached his dirty hands into the milk carton bin, grabbing as many as he could hold cradled in his arms, which, impressively, must have been about twenty cartons. Ice and water ran down the sleeves of his jacket, onto his pants, and down to the floor. He used the wet bottom folds of his dingy, green army jacket to wrap around a few more cartons.

Then he began giving away the milk to people waiting in line, muttering under his breath the whole while. I don't think it mattered if they wanted milk or not. He shoved the cartons into their hands and moved on to the next person anyway. Some folks walked away after getting their milk, others stayed in line saying "Thanks", but remained in line for something else, I guess.

Twice the man ran out of milk and he returned to the bin to get more. After the third refill, he reached in, but the bin was empty.

"GET MORE MILK!" he bellowed to no one in particular. He rubbed his wet hands across his face. He glared at the volunteers behind the table. "HEY, WE NEED MORE MILK OUT HERE!"

While most of the volunteers looked away at some spot on the wall next to them that they had just noticed needed their full attention, one woman eyed him and nodded, going off to get more milk like the man had so kindly suggested.

Out of milk, the guy stood for a moment, scratching at the dull red scar on the right side of his grizzled, unshaven face. Then squinting at the items to his left, he moved to a soda tub, reached deeply into the ice and cans for a couple of sodas. He pulled them out, dripping more ice and cold water on the floor, but mostly down his already soaked arms and coat sleeves.

"WHO WANTS A SODA!" he blared and looked up and down the line.

A woman with a small boy slowly raised her hand and he immediately thrust them towards her. She accepted the cans and the two went off to their hot meal. He stared at them as they departed and belched. I decided I would just wait quietly in line and pick up my own sodas.

More milk was brought out to refill the empty tub and, with this guy's assistance, the line was now moving along pretty well. I was only about fifth from the front, now, standing right next to the loud, wet man. Peering through the corners of my eyes, I noticed he was still dripping water from his coat sleeves as he stood looking behind me out to the throng in the hall. He was making some low, guttural sound, kind of like a cross between clearing a piece of food stuck in his windpipe and humming Jingle Bells, I think.

I peered at him again with my peripheral vision, as most of us are wont to do when someone's asking passersby for change outside of the donut shop or in front of the library or at the airport. He seemed harmless enough, but I hoped he would just let me quietly get my own sodas. I caught a little whiff of him, not too bad smelling, a little "natural," I suppose. Not really pungent, as his dirty, and now wet, army jacket and jeans suggested. His graying blond hair was long and a lot of it stuck up in tufts around his head. There was mud caked on his shoes, ragged Adidas Pro Models which had seen the last of any full-court basketball games, if any. One of the shoelaces had been replaced with a piece of double-laced kite string and there was a ragged hole near his right heel.

It's amazing how much you can really see with your peripheral vision!

He erupted again. "HEY, WILLIE! Get those folks moving through that line, for Pete's sake! This ain't no craft fair shopping party! THE FOOD'S GONNA GET COLD!"

I turned to look as he pointed to some guy standing next to the turkey and fixings, then he raised both hands over his head and wind-milled his arms in a great circle, like an airport runway operator waving planes from the runway into the terminal or something. The tufts of his scraggly hair seemed to move from the wind generated by his flailing arms. I took a step back, not wanting to get caught a glancing blow. Willie, if that was his name, kind of shrugged his shoulders and started helping people in line make their choices.

"CRIMINY!" the man muttered under his breath.

I moved up a space.

Suddenly, without turning his head, the man's soggy left arm reached out and promptly popped me on the chest. I think I made a little squeaky grunt sound in surprise, not a little bit scared of what I imagined was about to happen.

"HEY!" he shouted to no one in particular, as he stared straight ahead. "I know you!"

I was a little startled, to say the least, and thought for just a split second, "Man, what the hell kind of day am I having here?" I was a little too surprised, or maybe, petrified, to say anything as his hand remained affixed to the front of my shirt.

Then he turned his head towards me and eyed me with one eye squinting, one eye closed.

"Yeah, I know you. Daniel…" he was looking at my nametag. "Daniel…DAN HAMPTON…Galveon High, right? TRACK TEAM! GO TEAM! GO GALVEON! AAARRRGGGHHH!" He raised clenched fists towards the heavens as he roared.

Okay, so now I had to respond to this guy. Obviously he knew who I was.

I looked at him squarely, probably for the first time that day. I looked at his eyes, his face and I couldn't believe it!

It was Travis Waller, as I lived and breathed. If I was a little startled and surprised at first, I was truly floored then. Travis Waller! I tell you I couldn't believe it.

"Travis Waller." It was all I could get out. I whispered it like I had just witnessed some miracle. I think I said the words "Our baby" the same way the moment Jane was delivered, when the doctor pulled her from Marilyn's uterus to greet the world for the first time, crying and dripping with amniotic fluid. "Travis Waller," I repeated.

"Crap, man, HOW ARE YOU?" Travis Waller roared. He grabbed one of my hands with one of his cold wet ones and began pumping it up and down furiously. He wrapped his other big hand around my back and gave me a great big bear hug. Man, took the wind right out of me, which, of course I had hardly any left of anyway from the shock my system was experiencing.

I didn't know what to do as I just stood there breathing "Travis Waller" like I had been struck dumb or something. So, of course, I then said something truly idiotic. I mean what else could you expect?

"God. My hero. What the hell happened to you?"

"Hell, nothing's happened to me," he said, at first. Then rubbed his paw through his hair and said, "Well, yeah, you know stuff does happen. Aw hell, who knows?"

He was looking at me and I could see that he was sort of surprised himself, and maybe happy to see someone he knew. Maybe someone who knew him. Like I did.

"Travis, why don't you come have a seat with me and my little girl over there?" I pointed towards Jane who eyed the two of us. "That's Jane. She'd love to meet you." Oh my god, did I say that because Jane would love to meet a person like Travis, or a person in Travis's obvious less fortunate situation? What a jerk I am.

"Yeah, yeah. Okay, but just for a minute or two. I gotta lotta stuff to take care of." He turned and walked over towards where Jane was seated, grunting 'Hello' to everybody he passed, touching a shoulder here, grasping a hand there, nodding, waving, whispering, grunting— always that grunt.

"Yeah, sure," I thought. "He's probably got to meet his broker or something." Sometimes I can't stop my own sick, sarcastic mind.

I quickly grabbed three cans of soda from the tub. As I followed behind Travis Waller over to Jane, I had a moment to think about this.

Wow. Travis Waller. Who'd a thunk? And look at him. Crap, wonder what could have happened? How did things turn out this way for him? He still looked in pretty good shape under that jacket, but he sort of limped on his left leg. And it looked like he hadn't had a bath for a month. Maybe I could let Jane get him a plate of food or something. She might like that, but I don't know if that's appropriate behavior. Do I ask? What if he freaks or something?

And then my mind's eye flashed for just a second, a picture of this young god playing in a game of basketball out at the playground, the sun just starting to go down behind the park office building. There he was, running, flying, soaring. All movement, all grace. Swish.

Now as I stared at Travis Waller's back as he walked over to meet my eight-year-old daughter, I remembered how much this guy meant to me as I was growing up. How much Travis had helped me get through things without even knowing he had. How much I would always appreciate that. Him.

Travis pulled up a chair right next to Jane and, of course, I could see she was startled. She sat up straight as could be and looked around for me, relieved when I followed right behind Travis and sat down on the other side of her. I set the soda on the table for us. She looked at me for a second and then I saw her look at Travis from the corners of her eyes, just as I'm sure I did just a moment earlier. I put my arm around her.

"Jane, I would like you to meet someone. This is Travis Waller." I sort of bumped her elbow, causing her to reach up to shake his hand, still wet.

"Hello," she said to him, meekly.

"Well hello, Jane," he replied, pumping her hand up and down as he did with me. "Pleased to meet you, I'm sure. I knew your pa when he was just a pip-squeak, running around with snot in his nose."

Jane smiled at that thought. She looked back at me and grinned, rubbing her hand on her sweater. I hoped to dry them, not to wipe the imagined germs off. She pulled back the pop-top from her soda can and took a sip. Travis and I reached for a can and did the same.

"Jane, Travis and I sort of grew up together. We even went to the same schools."

"Really? To Preston Elementary School? Like me?"

Travis erupted. "HELL, YES!" he bellowed. "Preston Elementary, Northwest Junior High, and then GOOD OLD GALVEON HIGH. Are you going to go to Galveon?"

Jane nodded, hopefully.

"Me and your dad were track stars, Jane."

"Wow, were you, Daddy? A star? You know, you can't run very fast now. I bet I can beat you in a race. I'm one of the fastest in my class."

"HAHAHAHA!" Travis got a kick out of that. "Not too fast anymore, huh Hampton? Yeah, tell me about it! Got a bad knee myself, no more races, either, at least not the running kind."

He sat back in his seat and chugged the rest of his soda with his head tilted back at about a ninety-degree angle from his neck. Gulping sounds came from his throat as he downed it.

Jane, of course, had to try to do the same thing and spilled a bunch down her sweater, choking a bit as the soda bubbled up her nose. She jumped backwards in her seat, and dropped her can to the floor, spilling more soda as it rolled away under the table.

"Janie!" I cried and caught the rolling can with my foot.

"Sorry, Daddy!" she replied.

"Hey, don't worry, I got it," Travis said. He pulled a great wad of napkins and loose paper towels from one of his army jacket pockets. "No big deal. Accidents happen."

He plopped a bunch of napkins on Jane's chest before ducking under the table to wipe up the rest of the spill. In a few seconds he had the mess all dried up, picked up Jane's soda can and placed it back on the table in front of her. It was empty. As Jane and I both mumbled our "Thanks for cleaning up", he took the wet paper towels, rolled them up in a ball and put them back in the same pocket they had come from.

"Soda's empty, want another?" He looked at Jane. Then he and Jane looked at me.

I shrugged my shoulders. "It's okay, but try to drink most of it this time."

"Daddy!" Jane squealed. She got up, but Travis stopped her.

"You just sit here with your Pop. I'll get it for you. Orange, again, or something different?"

"Travis, you don't have to, I'll get it," I said to him as he got up.

"No problem, it's my treat. But you'll both owe me one." He placed his hand on Jane's head. "You both have to promise to be back here next year." And he walked off to get the soda.

"Orange, again!" Jane called after him. He raised a hand in acknowledgment without turning around.

"Man," I thought. "Travis must be a regular to this thing."

I started to wonder what happened to him during the rest of the holidays, but I didn't really want to let myself wonder what happened to him during the rest of the holidays, the rest of the year. What did he do? How did this happen?

"Daddy," Jane was pulling at my arm. "Sorry about the spill."

I shrugged my shoulders again. "It's all right, Jane. Like Travis said, accidents happen."

"Did you really go to school with him, Daddy?" she asked. "Were you friends and everything? What's wrong with him, Daddy? He's really nice and everything, but is he, unh, homeless, or something?

Where does he live? Why's he like that and you're, I mean, we're not? Is he here to eat, is he hungry?"

I realized I didn't have to wonder about those things as long as Jane was around to ask the questions for me.

"I don't know all the answers, Jane," I told her, putting my arm back around her again. "Travis and I did go to the same schools and played at the same parks and stuff. But he was older than me and we weren't really-really friends, like you and your friend, Erica. I mean, we didn't go to each other's birthday parties, or sleep over at each other's house, or play at the park together and all that. Well, I guess we did play at the park together, but sort of like different sports and different times. Mostly I got to watch Travis play a lot. And he was great."

"Better at sports than you, Dad?"

"Oh, yeah," I said sincerely. "Way better. I guess he taught me how to play sports and do all kinds of things that I never thought I could do myself."

"Like my third grade teacher, Ms. Enders?" I knew by that comparison that Jane understood some of the awe in which I held Travis Waller in my life. Ms. Enders was her favorite.

"Well, sort of like Ms. Enders, but not really," I tried to explain. "Travis Waller was not a teacher and didn't really try to show me how to do things and how to be, but just because I got to see how HE was and how HE did things and how HE tried so hard, then I wanted to do those things too, like him."

"You mean he was your idol, Daddy?" Jane asked with eight-year-old innocence. I swear, out of the mouths of babes. "Ms. Enders said it was okay if Michael Jordan was Todd Bruner's idol, but that Martin Luther King, Jr. could be a good idol, too. She said we all kinda pick our own."

Travis was just now making his way back with another can of soda for Jane. Along the way I had watched him stop at the one of the huge mashed potato serving pots, grab the server's giant ladle and give the potatoes a swift and vigorous stir. Then he had helped move a large table away from the food line so that some old guy in a wheel chair could get right up to the front to be served.

"Yeah, Jane. I picked Travis Waller. It was a good pick, I think."

As Travis came up to us he gave Jane the soda and pulled another wad of paper towels out his pocket for her, too. "Just in case," he mumbled.

"Thank you very much," she said to Travis.

"You're very welcome," he replied and bowed.

He looked at me and stuck out his grimy paw.

"Look, Dan, I got to get going here, uh, got some things to do. It was real nice seeing you again, maybe we can hook up sometime."

Wait a second, I thought to myself. I can't just say 'so long' after so many years. There were too many things I wanted to say to Travis, too many things I wanted to know about him. Too many things I wanted him to know about me.

I let Travis help me so much without even a thank you in return. And I never helped him, never did anything for him. Maybe I could have done something. Maybe I could have helped HIM. I picked Travis Waller to be my idol. A good pick, I told Jane. I needed to tell him. He was my hero, no matter what had happened.

Instead, I just stood and shook his hand. I grasped it firmly as Travis did in return. A strong grip, I always knew. I looked in his eyes and they were strong, too. Clear and intense.

"It was great to see you, again, Travis. And I'm glad that you got to meet my daughter. We really should keep in touch. I need to hook up with you. There's a lot to catch up on."

"Yeah, you're right," he replied, releasing my hand. "I do want to catch up. To a lot of things."

"Jeez, Travis," I told him. "From what I remember everyone was always trying to catch up to you."

"Yeah," he mumbled, looking down and shuffling his feet. "Ain't it a kick the way things just turn out sometimes?" He glanced up and smiled at me.

I smiled back. "It's always better if you have someone around who's always there to help."

After a quick quiet moment, he replied. "Thanks, I guess. Hey I gotta get back."

"No," I said. "Thank you."

Travis reached down and shook Jane's hand, too.

"Gotta go, Jane. It sure was a treat to meet you. You spill soda better'n any other kid I know."

Now Jane got the smile.

"Thanks, Travis. It was nice to meet you and thanks for the soda." Then Jane looked at him with a serious expression. "Are you going to eat now?"

"Jane!" I scolded. "You don't need to ask that. Hey, don't worry about it, Travis, go on and do what you need to do." I took Jane's hand and she got up to leave with me.

"No problem here," he said to me. He turned to Jane. "Heck no, Jane, I don't eat until everyone else is done. During cleanup I make sure all of the volunteers get some grub or soda or a treat or something. But only after the guests are done. That's why we do this every year. Right now I'm gonna help dish out some of that bird and Thanksgiving stuff. Line's not moving too quick. Gotta take care of business, again. But it sure was nice to meet you."

"What?!" Jane whined in her favorite eight-year-old whine. "You get to serve food? Me and Daddy didn't get to."

Travis stopped to look at Jane, then me. "Whadya mean you 'didn't get to'? Who said so? Did I say so? Do you want to still?"

"Well," I stammered. "When we got here, some guy named Fred said he had enough servers. But that's okay, we got to help some and Jane did a lot of stuff, right, Jane?"

"Yes," Jane replied. "But, no, Daddy, we really wanted to serve food to the hungry people, remember? We really wanted to do that most of all. We did." She took hold of Travis' coat sleeve. "Can we help you, Travis? Do you need help?"

"Shit, Jane, I mean, shoot, Jane. Sorry 'bout that," he said. "Of course I need help. Fred Parkerson needs more help than I do, though. Hahahahahaa! Come on with me, we can always use more. What about it, Dad. It's okay?"

"Hell, yes, Travis," I replied. "That's why we're here. To help. But how the heck can you do this?"

"Whadya mean 'HOW THE HEY-ECK CAN I DO THIS!'" he bellowed. "I freakin' run this damn thing THAT'S why the heck I can! I got placed at the damn public health department a few years back after some time and treatment I went through. We do this every Thanksgiving. I took over the whole shebang about five years ago. Used to eat here myself for a coupla years, until I figured out what to do with myself. And Fred's just my assistant, no matter what he thinks. You two come on with me."

I followed Travis, who walked hand-in-hand with Jane over to the food tables and the other servers. I know I must have just been shaking my head in wonder, too surprised to think coherently.

Here was my daughter, holding hands with my childhood idol I hadn't seen for a zillion years, who not ten minutes ago I thought looked so bad I would have sworn under oath to be just another lost degenerate. Now, I just found out he happens to be running the largest, most charitable Thanksgiving Day community event in the whole county. I couldn't believe it.

Travis led Jane and me behind the row of servers, busily ladling food onto guests' reaching plates. Turkey, stuffing, all kinds of potatoes, vegetables, beans, rice, spaghetti. All kinds of food. And hungry guests. A great long line of kids, adults, and families with babies. Disheveled, in suits, pushing carts of stuff too valuable to leave unattended, and wearing t-shirts too thin for the weather outside the Hall.

The noise inside the Hall had risen greatly as warm food, music and laughter all added to the mix. There were children giggling, people talking, old friends greeting, and many people sharing a meal together. Some did so in silence.

Travis seemed to know them all. He never stopped muttering, bellowing, cajoling, laughing. "Good to see you, Pat." "HEY, you need another tray here!" "Well take care of yourself, Jules, and that pretty baby, too." "Thanks for helping out." "Gina, help Ms. Hendon over here with this plate. Thanks." "Don't just stand there HALF ASLEEP, RAY, keep the line moving." "Appreciate you coming down today." "What are them WILD KIDS up to these days?!" "Hahahahahah! I TOLD you that would DO IT, DIDN'T I?" "Glad you could help."

Everyone he passed took at least a moment out for Travis Waller. "Hey, Travis, this turkey almost looks good enough to eat!" "Who's the kid, Travis, your date?" "Thanks for getting that stool for us, it was just what we needed." "Did you hear that man crying earlier?" "Great job, Travis." "Need more squash here." "Thank you, Travis."

In the midst of all of the commotion, Travis Waller stopped and turned to Jane and me. He eyeballed us for a moment. I could feel his brain working. Then he seemed to reach a decision.

"Seems like we got it covered pretty good right here, but I've got the perfect place for you two. Come on."

He took us to the end of the food tables, to the last table, where another long, long line of guests awaited. I could see the line getting longer as more guests piled onto the end. The dessert area! There were so many varieties of cakes and pumpkin, cherry, apple, and rhubarb pies. There was pudding and other treats, too.

Travis bent over to speak to Jane. He raised his voice even more to be heard over the din.

"Now all these people here, Jane, they want the perfect treat to top off their Thanksgiving meal. You know, MAKE IT SPECIAL! There's all kinds of good stuff here, too. What's your favorite dessert?"

He tilted his head to Jane's. "JELL-O?! With or without whipped cream? WITH? Well, all right then, I know just where you should be. COME ON!"

He smiled to me as he rose to lead Jane over to a spot where another woman was loading up bowls full of jiggling, brightly colored squirming Jell-O. Travis said something to the woman, who promptly plopped a chef's hat on Jane's head and slipped a loose fitting glove over Jane's left hand. She added a large spoon and a can of spray whipped cream in Jane's right. Jane looked at me and I would have heard her squeal of delight over any roar of sound. She dove right into her new job, a plop of Jell-O and a jolt of whipped cream on every plate that passed.

"HAVING FUN, JANE?" Travis shouted to her now.

"THIS IS PERFECT!" she cried. "You're my Hero!"

"Hey, you're mine!" Travis said, giving her a quick hug, which she returned with obvious joy. "Now give 'em something sweet, won't you?!"

Travis left her with a twinkle in his eye and one in hers as well.

He stepped back to me and I placed a hand on his shoulder.

"You know, Travis," I said to him. "Now you're going to be Jane's hero for the rest of her life, too."

He smiled at me. "There's no bigger hero than Dad." And then he surprised me with a quick hug. "Damn, it's good to see you, someone from home again. Come check me out at the county building, okay? I'd like to hear what's been going on. Now go on and help your kid—I got things to do."

"Christ, me too," I told him as we nodded good-bye. "Thanks for everything."

And later as I stood there with Jane, finally doing that nice thing we both had wanted so badly to do, looking at all of the faces of the folks as they passed, somewhere behind me I could hear Travis' voice bellowing out.

I thought to myself, "If there's no bigger hero than Dad, then what does that make Dad's hero?"

And, for a very brief second, I could feel that eight-year-old boy feeling, that familiar settling of my heart, in my soul, I'm not sure what. Admiration. The honest respect for another person, friend perhaps, maybe hero even, knowing for just that moment, at least, that things were truly in balance.

Jane smiled up to me, as if reading my thoughts, a feat which I will look back on when I'm old and gray as something she would do many, many times. Usually at just the right moment.

"Travis Waller is a good idol, Daddy. He made a great Thanksgiving for a lot of people."

I smiled back at her and nodded.

THE MATTER OF MARILYN

Based on the fable "The Hunter and the Woodman": A Hunter, not very bold, was searching for the tracks of a Lion. He asked a man felling oaks in the forest if the man had seen any marks of the lion or knew where his lair was. "I will show you the Lion himself," said the man. The Hunter, turning very pale from fear, replied, "No, thank you. I did not ask that; it is his tracks only I am in search of, not the Lion himself."

The moral of the fable is: The hero is brave in deeds as well as words.

J ingle bell, jingle bell, jingle bell rock."

Marilyn sang aloud, tapping time on her computer keyboard. She'd been doing this all day long, her singing growing louder and louder (and more off key) as Christmas Eve wore on.

"Ah, Christmas," she sighed abruptly to the empty office cubicles. She glanced at the clock on the wall above her: eleven o'clock and the budgets still weren't balanced. She wondered if she would ever get this paperwork done. "Oh well, that's Christmas in the health care business."

Marilyn proceeded to supply her own lyrics to 'Rudolph'. "I'm balancing county budgets…Eleven o'clock p.m.… I'll have to keep on working…'Til I'm old and gray and then…time to do them all over… it doesn't really matter why…just so I work my butt off…then I can go home and cry…"

And Marilyn almost did break down and cry right then. Almost, but she didn't. She had pretty much cried herself out over the last few weeks and had enough of that.

Yes, she had cried. Marilyn wasn't even quite sure why, because she made sure she never spent too much time analyzing it. When she cried a bit more, she felt guilty about doing that, too because, after all, she alone was the one who had allowed her work to become so important. No one could help the fact Christmas came along and interfered. Yes, her husband and kids, with Marilyn's blessing, decided to head back east ahead of her, so what? Marilyn would be there soon enough. Maybe even before the New Year, who knows? Why spoil their fun? Wasn't that being totally unselfish?

But, of course Marilyn did allow herself to think about it too much. All the time, in fact. As good as she was getting these budgets balanced, why couldn't she get her life balanced? Too much work, too little family time. Too much family time, too much work undone. Marilyn was having a hard time making it all work. Damn it, no one had told her it was going to be this hard!

Of course, then she would end up feeling sorry for herself which would make her cry even more.

So here the hard working civil servant sat, trying to get the fifth rendition of the late State budgets approved. Marilyn wasn't proud of being late, but she was very proud that, under her direction, the program had grown so large over the last couple of years. The budgets had grown larger as well and become more and more difficult.

It was worth it, all of it was worth it. It was for the kids. More benefited this year from the medical and dental and housing services than the last, with a greater reach projected after that. Who knew how many more? It was worth it, right?

Marilyn punched in fifteen thousand more dollars for additional computer equipment. Oh yeah, the State was going to like that one.

"Silent night, holy night, all is calm. Too calm." Marilyn stopped herself. "It's too quiet in here."

When had she started talking to herself so continuously? Did she do this when the staff was here? She couldn't remember. Marilyn definitely carried out long, drawn out conversations with herself while working lately it seemed.

"Is it worth it?" Marilyn asked herself aloud, her hands splayed out flat on the keyboard. "Does it matter? Do I matter? What do I get out of it? Pay—fair. Honor, glory—some, whatever. But what else? Do the kids benefit? Are they thankful? What about my own kids? And

Dan? What do they get out of it? Less of me, for sure, but more income, more stuff. In the end it's all worth it. "

But she just wasn't always sure. Not sure at all. Everything had been reduced to a muddled mass of data, numbers, dollars, statistics, state, federal, county mandates, and bureaucracy. Plus a little more strain at home. Dan was a great dad and husband. He covered for her all the time lately. No, she wasn't sure any more if any of it mattered.

Why was she doing this anyway?

And over the last few days, Marilyn had been so tired. She blamed it on the long hours. Those hours plus the limited breaks and food always eaten on the run. By the time she returned to their empty townhouse she literally flopped onto the living room couch and fell fast asleep, hardly enough energy left to grab a blanket.

Marilyn yawned. If only she could just close her eyes for a moment or two to recharge her internal batteries. That would help give her the energy to finish this up and get on home. Just a minute, maybe five tops, but that was all.

She sighed, shook her head to clear her thoughts, and set about the budgets again.

Marilyn positioned her fingers on the keyboard and stared at the spreadsheet displayed on the monitor. The hairs on the back of her neck stood on end and a chill rolled down her spine, causing an unexpected shiver.

"What was that?" she asked herself. Marilyn sat quietly for a moment, straining her ears. Had she heard something on the other side of the office, near the back entrance? She listened. No, nothing.

She sighed another time, realizing she'd been holding her breath.

"Darn it," she said aloud. "Get a grip on yourself, Marilyn Anne. Maybe I just ought to ki—!"

There it was again. Someone WAS there! In the office! She froze for a split second, her thoughts reeling in momentary panic.

Everybody knew it was too damned dangerous downtown. You read about crazy things happening all the time. Everyone told her to be careful, but she always listened to them with only one ear. Nothing would ever happen to her, come on. Sure, she'd been frightened before, each time a simple over-reaction on her part. But, for some reason, this time she felt differently, nerve endings all screaming at once.

Sweat formed on her brow and her breathing stopped again. It was Christmas Eve, by God. She was certain not another county employee was in the building, no security, no co-workers, no help. Oh crap.

The noise picked up. Whoever or whatever it was, was going through the cupboards lining the back wall, where the coffee and all of the lunchroom supplies were kept.

Marilyn glanced at the clock again. 11:15. Why the heck had she stayed so late? Her eyes darted about, a place to hide! Under the desk? Oh no, the computer! If she left it on whoever it was would know she was here. Hell, they probably knew already since she had all of the office lights blaring. If she turned the thing off, the noise would be loud in the quiet of the near-empty office. Either way, her visitor—visitors?—would know she was in there, somewhere.

The rustling came toward her direction. Another supply cabinet slammed, a box ripped open. Who was it?

The police! Marilyn dropped out of her chair to her knees and began inching over to the phone on the desk behind her, Stacey's desk. The police station was just two minutes away. She slid as quietly as she possibly could. A drop of sweat stung as it rolled into her left eye, then out again, down her cheek. No, the sweat turned to tears. Marilyn was hardly aware she had been stifling sobs, not wanting to cry out, but the tears didn't stop.

Crouching at the desk now, Marilyn hesitated. It had become quiet and Stacey's cubicle walls blocked her from being seen from the rear of the office. Marilyn drew a deep breath and reached out a hand to pick up the phone.

"Oh, I don't think I'd do that." The voice boomed in her head.

She'd been found.

By some old man. Dirty clothes, white haired, a mud-stained knit hat pulled down to his eyebrows. The hat was too muddy to determine its true colors. He wore one filthy tennis shoe, one black boot. But the eyes, bright blue and clear, almost twinkled in the light.

"Let's not be too rash here," he said. He didn't sound too threatening, but you couldn't be sure in the city.

"What are you doing in here?" Marilyn stood, not wanting to appear frightened. She put the phone back, but didn't let go of it and never once took her eyes off of his. Could she even if she wanted to?

"Uh, well, I was hungry," the man replied gruffly. He reached up to pull off his hat, which made Marilyn flinch involuntarily and recoil in fear. His eyes still held her but he didn't try to harm her. His long white hair fell free just to the collar of his tattered and grubby coat. Marilyn could see that his eyebrows matched his bushy white hair.

Something seemed odd about the intruder as she took a better look at him. Yes. It was his hair—white and clean. And his hands too—spotless. His clothes, hat, shoes, all filthy, but it seemed the man himself was not.

"Saw the light up here from down on the street. Thought maybe a party or something was going on." He smiled. "I like parties. Usually you can pretty much get your fill of free food. Can't often stay to eat, though, just pack up and shove on. One of the side doors was unlocked. Why are you here so late, alone?"

That sounded like something her boss might ask also if he knew she was here working on Christmas Eve.

"Listen, there's no party and you have to leave this building immediately." Her initial feelings of fear dissipated and now she was feeling angry. Still a bit afraid, but getting mad, too. "And why were you going through those cabinets?"

"I told you, Marilyn, I was hungry, looking for something to eat. You pack a dinner, midnight snack or anything like that?"

"How the hell do you know my name?" Marilyn asked him. "And I'm sorry, but you do have to leave." She nodded towards the back exit.

His head dropped, shoulders slumped. The man heaved a deep sigh.

Marilyn, as was her nature, relented. "Well, okay, look," she told him. "I do have half a turkey sandwich left if you want it. And an orange, too."

His bright eyes lifted and shined, meeting hers and dazzling her again.

"I knew you'd come through, Marilyn," the old man smiled, now laughing. "Ha, ha, ho, ho, ho…"

Marilyn went back to her workstation, shaking her head. "This guy is nuts," she mumbled softly aloud. She pulled her nylon lunch sack out of her bottom drawer and rummaged around before pulling out her half-eaten sandwich, an orange, and then, after just a slight hesitation, a small bag of Oreo's.

"Dessert!" Marilyn said to the visitor, turning to hand him his meager Christmas dinner.

But he wasn't there. She looked about.

Great, where'd he go? And then Marilyn heard him, back at the rear door again.

"Step lively now," she heard him say. To whom? And then, "Come on. All of you, come in, follow me."

All of you?!

And then he returned. And behind him were others; ten, fifteen, even more behind them. Marilyn could see most of them were families—fathers, mothers, children, and babies. They were bundled up in blankets, old sleeping bags, ripped jackets, bath towels, anything in an attempt to keep out the winter cold. Some of them dirty, some not. Some wafted a bad stench. Others stared blankly ahead, while the children looked about with wide eyes. They had one thing in common. Each and every one of them looked tired, worn out. Actually they had two things in common, Marilyn saw: they were also all smiling now as the old guy led them over to her.

"Here," the white haired visitor simply said, presenting the new arrivals to her with a short wave of his hand. Then he turned to face the group. "This is Marilyn Hampton."

"What!" Marilyn blurted out. "How did…?"

"They're hungry, Marilyn," he cut her off. "Hungry, tired, cold, lonely. All of them. What can we do with them?"

It took but a single moment of hesitation before Marilyn knew what to do because that was what Marilyn did. She helped them.

"Come," she told them all, holding her arms wide as if to draw them all into her and hold them. "Here, come with me."

And then Marilyn strode off with them following, off to where she knew the supply of blankets were for the clinics, cases of canned formula, donated diapers, boxes of crackers and stored cheeses, emergency supplies of canned goods, clothes, fruit, and bottled water. She threw open supply cabinets and started ripping boxes open.

"Here!" she called out, throwing supplies this way and that. "Take these, open them up, and pass them out. Make sure you each get enough, and then pass the rest on. Take these pots. Go to the sink to fill them up for coffee and tea. Here you go. Pass out these plates and napkins. The bottles are there. Ooh, cut that up. And here's more formula."

And Marilyn helped them all, smiling, touching, hugging, holding children, babies, and adults. She wanted to feed them, nurture them, and keep them warm. Marilyn was in her element, one hundred percent pure Marilyn. Nothing else mattered at that moment but being here, helping these people that needed her help.

The night became most joyous for all of them: safe, calm, and bright.

The watch startled her when the hourly alarm went off. "Beep, beep, beep, beep, beep!" She glanced at it.

"It's midnight!" Marilyn yelled out without thinking. "Christmas! It's Christmas!"

They all stopped and looked at Marilyn. She was radiant in Christmas cheer. The budgets were long forgotten for now. Then the entire group smiled at her even more brightly, wishing her a very Merry Christmas as they were all filled with the spirit of Marilyn's giving, Marilyn's Christmas.

The old man came over to her, popped a last bit of cheese and cracker into his mouth.

"Merry Christmas, Marilyn," he spoke softly to her. He reached his arms around her and they hugged tightly. "Look around you, Marilyn, the faces. You've helped them all. You help them all the time. You matter."

"Yes," she sighed into his thick white hair. "You know, sometimes I think I do."

"You do," he replied.

Marilyn drew back and looked into his eyes—so clear, so bright.

"Christmas music!" she cried out suddenly. "Oh, if only we had Christmas music!" She broke away. Wasn't there a radio in Robert's desk? He was always listening to it!

"No, Marilyn, wait!" The white-haired intruder called to her. "Listen, we have music, it's here. We have it."

She stopped and then she heard it. Yes, Marilyn did hear it!

Music, beautiful, full, rich voices. It was a children's choir singing so clearly. And the sound grew, running through the entire office. The rich sound broadened the smiles of all and enriched the joy and warmth of the sudden Christmas gathering. Music and the sound of voices singing filled the air.

"It's beautiful," Marilyn cried. "Wonderful!" The others nodded in agreement. "But where's it coming from? Where's the stereo?"

"Here," the old man told her. "Here's your music."

And he pulled the cords to the blinds behind him. All along the long office wall others suddenly pulled up every one of the blinds, exposing the city streets below.

The music grew, the voices expanding. The sound became so unbelievably magnificent and filled Marilyn completely to her very soul.

"Come, Marilyn, come," her old visitor called to her. "Come see and hear the wonder. They all need to tell you."

And she went to the wall of open windows and looked out.

Down below, the streets were filled with children lined all along every street. They were crammed into every doorway, at every corner, every alleyway, and every driveway. Children as far as she could see: wonderful, beautiful, singing children. Each face turned up to her, reaching up to Marilyn with the extraordinary sound of their voices. Singing to her, joyous music for her.

"They sing 'Merry Christmas' to you, Marilyn," the old gent said, his eyes twinkling. "Because you make a difference for them."

And that was when something deep in Marilyn's heart stirred because it was there that she knew she mattered.

NEO-HOMELESS

Based on the fable "The Dancing Monkeys": A Prince had monkeys trained to dance. Once arrayed in the rich clothing and masks of man, the dancing monkeys were a wonderful spectacle for the Prince's guests. But, during one performance, a mischievous courtier decided to throw a handful of nuts at the stage. The monkeys, seeing the nuts, stopped their dancing and became, as they indeed always were, monkeys, pulling off their masks and ripping their clothes as they fought one another for the nuts. Amid the audience's laughter and Prince's shame, the show ended.

The moral of the fable: Not everything is what it appears to be.

Yes, can I comment?"

"Please do, Neal."

Neal sat up straight in his chair and looked at the previous speaker. He quickly reached up to pull his royal blue paisley tie straight and tight. He really looked all business in his coal gray double-breasted suit coat and matching pleated slacks, white button down shirt and tie. Nice.

"Rachel, you are a fantastic person. I think your skills and experience will land you a job in no time." He paused for a moment. "Any company should be happy to have you as an employee; they just have to figure out how your skills translate. You have to just keep trying and keep positive."

Rachel smiled very appreciatively and the rest of the employment training group nodded their heads in agreement.

"Thank you, Neal," Rachel replied. "And I think the same goes for you, too. And while I do get what you said, it still feels good to hear it once in a while."

"Yes," someone in the back called out. "Instead of the same old rejection calls."

From someone else: "Or no calls at all."

The meeting ended a few minutes later. The small group left the EDD—Employment Development Department—office and headed to the parking lot. Neal walked a few steps behind them. Rachel stopped and turned.

"Hey, Neal," she told him as he walked up. "That really was a nice thing to say. I wasn't just saying that."

"Yeah, Neal," another person said. "You're always so positive and helpful."

"I try, guys," Neal shyly responded. "Thanks."

"Hey, we're all going out for some breakfast at Alfred's," Rachel offered. "For some reason Ms. Alphonse didn't have the usual donuts and hot coffee this morning. Want to come?"

"Oh, no, no thanks." Neal politely deferred. "I have some errands to run this morning. You know, gotta get those apps and resumes out there. Maybe next time."

"Okay, great. Well, have a great day and see you later. Good luck!"

"Yeah, thanks and you, too."

The rest of the group wished him well and moved off to their cars. Neal again lagged behind them, then turned and started walking off. But Rachel stopped and called to him again.

"Hey, Neal," she asked. "Do you need a ride or something?"

"Huh?" He looked at her. "No, I'm good. My car's parked over in C-lot. Thanks, though. See you this afternoon maybe. Or if not, next Thursday." And with that he turned and walked towards C-lot, two lots over.

But, once Neal reached C-lot, he did not enter it to find his car. Instead he crossed the street and walked down another school driveway. Towards the back end of the driveway were six large garbage dumpsters. His two-door Hyundai commuter car was parked behind the last dumpster. Neal took a quick peek at the front windshield: no ticket. He smiled, knowing he escaped the parking fee again.

With another glance around before unlocking the vehicle, Neal opened the driver side door and reached in to flick the trunk lever. Walking to the rear of the car and removing his coat, he lifted the trunk lid and pulled out a black vinyl garment bag. Neal unzipped the bag and removed a hanger from within. After placing his coat on the hanger, he carefully placed the coat into the garment bag and re-zipped.

Neal temporarily hung the garment bag on the raised trunk lid and removed a box marked "Sweaters". He rifled through the folded sweaters and took out a pale blue v-neck wool sweater. The box was then returned next to the other two boxes that made up the rest of his entire wardrobe. Neal laid the garment bag back smoothly on top of them, not wanting his only two suit coats to get wrinkled.

§ § §

It was after ten o'clock and Neal was hungry. He drove over to the Starbucks on the other side of town, right next to Shawson's Industrial Park. The ten o'clock break crowd would be there for a little while longer and he wanted to get there before they trooped on back to work.

When Neal arrived, he parked a little ways past the rear of the Starbucks storefront, next to a large maintenance van. Hopefully, the van would be parked for a while.

Neal reached behind his car seat and grabbed the folded grocery bag that contained his treasured Dell laptop and AC charge unit. Neal took these out then replaced the bag on top of his white toiletry case to keep that hidden. Inside were his toothbrush, toothpaste, a small bar of nameless soap, plus three other paper-wrapped bars. It also held a small container of sanitized paper wipes, three disposable razors, and a small wash cloth faded into an unrecognizable color from too many hand-washings. A guy had to look presentable! Neal tucked the laptop and cords under one arm. Before leaving the car, he grabbed the used Starbucks grande-sized coffee cup from his dashboard cup holder. With one last pat of his breast pocket to make sure his cell phone was there, exited the vehicle.

Only one of the six outdoor tables was occupied at the Starbucks. A couple of guys, both wearing long-sleeved white shirts and ties with company IDs pinned to their shirt pockets were on a coffee break from their jobs in the industrial park.

Neal placed his stuff down at an empty table, connected the power adaptor unit to the laptop even though there wasn't anywhere to plug it in out there, and opened up the laptop. No sense in turning the thing on since the battery no longer worked. He pretended to study the blank screen for a minute or so, taking a few phony sips from his empty coffee cup, and waited another bogus minute to enjoy the coffee. From his outdoor seat he could see there was a line of people waiting to place their orders inside the store, with another four people lingering in the rear by the barista's pick up area. Neal faked another sip and waited patiently.

Ah. There. A worker brought out a tray of free sample tasters — small cups of the latest, newest coffee flavor of the season. Emphasis, as far as Neal was concerned, on the "free". He stood up.

"Hey, fellas," he called over to the two guys seated at the other table. "You going to be here a minute? Mind keeping an eye on my laptop while I run in?"

Yeah, sure, they nodded.

"Great, be right back."

Neal entered the Starbucks, took a place at the end of the line and stared momentarily at the menu board on the wall behind the pastry shelves. Then he walked over to the tray of free samples near the register, said a polite "Excuse me, ma'am" to the woman placing her coffee order. Neal smiled at the young man behind the register but the employee wasn't even paying attention so he reached over to grab a couple of the small cups.

Neal exited the store, nodded a quick thanks to the two guys sitting outside and resumed his seat. Taking the lid off his grande coffee cup, he poured the contents of the two samples in, and replaced the lid. Neal took a real sip this time. Mmmmm, still hot.

With a smile, Neal closed the laptop, picked everything up except his trash and headed back into the coffee shop. There was an empty small table near the rear with an outlet right behind the seat. Settling in, Neal plugged in his laptop. He took his cell phone out of his shirt pocket and placed it next to his computer. No sense in turning that one on though, his service lapsed weeks ago. No, the cell phone was all for show, just to keep in practice.

Neal raised the laptop screen. With power now, the machine booted up and his job search began. First, he checked his free email address, a temporary introductory offer the internet provider gave to new subscribers for up to 90 days. Thankfully it wasn't going to end for him for a few more weeks. After that, something else would turn up.

No messages from prospective employers. Hell, no messages at all, except the usual junk advertisements. Right. He deleted them all.

A couple of tables over, Neal noticed a young woman sip from her extra-large, venti cup while she looked after a child. The girl was maybe two or three years old with a small milk and pastry. The pastry was a huge bear claw almost the same size as the child's head. The child did a great job of devouring half of it, but quickly lost interest and promptly sat on the floor reading a small plastic book.

"Sarah, finish your milk and breakfast. Nanny has to go to the store."

"I'm done, Nanny," the kid replied, not looking up from the book.

"Are you sure you're done?" Nanny (short for Nancy? the kid's nanny?) asked. "Did you drink all your milk?"

"All gone." The kid stood up. "Will you read this book to me?" She handed the book to Nanny.

"Yes, yes, but later. Now put on your coat and let's go."

Nanny handed the child her yellow vest and put the book in the large canvas bag at her feet. The empty milk carton and the pastry were deposited into a small, brown Starbucks bag. Neal's heart sank when he saw this, but instantly brightened when the nanny picked up the bag and dropped it into the trashcan right next to where Neal sat. Soon the two gathered their things and left.

Most of the coffee break crowd had filed out while Neal sat mesmerized by the nanny and child, honestly more interested by the kid's half uneaten pastry. Neal moved over to the register, grabbing the last sample cup on the tray. He smiled, again unnoticed, at the clerk and drained the cup.

Back at his table, Neal finished the coffee he collected. He walked over to the condiment area and removed the lid from his cup, grabbing five raw sugar packets and a wooden stir stick. Then Neal reached for the whole milk pitcher, opened the spout and poured milk into his cup. The cup was almost full when the pitcher ran out. He proceeded to sprinkle a load of cocoa powder from a silver. Neal put the sugar packets into his pocket for later while stirring his chocolate milk mixture and finally replaced the cup's plastic cover. Stepping back to his seat, Neal stopped to casually drop his used stir stick into the trash can, and with one deft motion, pulled the child's garbage bag out with his other hand away from the employees' line of sight. Breakfast!

Neal spent the next hour or so following up on potential jobs over the Internet and enjoying his hastily prepared and 100% free of charge breakfast.

§ § §

As the noon hour approached, Neal thought to go check his mailbox. Maybe he'd received a response to one of his job applications the old-fashioned way: through the postal service. There had been no responses on line. Worse yet, he also hadn't found any new opportunities to apply for.

He checked the dashboard clock. There was still an hour-plus before the job faire sponsored by EDD started. This was going to be held outdoors at the City Center Plaza thirty minutes away, plenty of time to check his mail slot before heading over.

Neal pulled his car out of the Starbucks parking lot and headed north on Industrial Park Way. The park was only a couple of years old. Not all of the buildings had occupants yet. He reached the north end of the parkway, passing a couple of vacant lots mixed in with some smaller one-floor offices. Hard packed dirt lots were strewn with almost leafless scrub bushes and human trash. Bits of glass from broken bottles glittered in the noontime sun and windblown white plastic bags rolled lazily about like modern-day tumbleweed. In the middle of this area was a dilapidated gas station, no longer in use and scheduled to be torn down and rebuilt into some fancy office building at some point in the near future. Just not TOO soon Neal hoped.

He pulled his car around the back of the station, parked and got out. His toiletry case and bath towel with him, Neal headed over to a locked door which led to the old co-ed bathroom. Without hesitating, Neal grabbed the metal lock and pulled down hard. The lock popped open. It wasn't really locked at all.

A few weeks ago he had come across this spot looking for a quiet place to take a quick nap out of public view and patrolling police cars. It was truly a very lucky day for Neal when he found the lock on this door wasn't fastened properly. Inside, lo and behold, he discovered more miracles as the toilet facility still worked. There was running cold water, but no hot, and a fairly respectably clean sink, at least by gas station standards. After a couple of visits he rigged the lock clasp when he departed, making it look like it was locked. This kept unwanted guests out of his private bathroom. This time he entered and gave himself a quick wash and shave, spruced up his hair, and took care of nature's business. With all this done, he replaced his toiletry items back in their case and stepped out, closing the bathroom door tight. Neal set the lock clasp so that with a cursory look one would think that the lock was set.

Neal felt refreshed, but hungry. He needed to get over to the job faire before whatever snacks they provided ran out, but he still had to check his mailbox.

Neal went around to the front of the vacant gas station. Beside the entrance was a metal mail delivery box. On that luckiest of days when Neal chanced upon this place, he also found recent junk mail in the box, which meant the post office was still delivering to the vacant building. That day, he not only found his very own bathroom, but his very own mail delivery site too. The gas station's address was on all of his applications, freebie offerings, and anything else requiring a real mailing location. As usual, this time there was only more junk mail.

No important job offers or vacation getaways. Oh well. He knew a job offer would be coming his way soon; had to be.

Neal got into his car and drove over to the Center Plaza and the outdoor job faire. Should his luck hold out again today, he'd get a little something to snack on. They always offered refreshments at these things—an enticement to get folks to attend. As if the lure of a job offer wasn't enough.

§ § §

Driving around the downtown area, Neal found an empty corner parking space in a pharmacy store parking lot just three blocks off the Plaza. He didn't want to park too close in case one of his nosy employment development group friends decided to check out his current mobile living arrangements. Hey, shit happened and people just needed to understand that. You didn't have to like it, but no one else needed to know about it either.

Neal got out and took off his sweater, carefully folded and replaced it in his sweater box. He put on his double-breasted suit coat, grabbed his portfolio file and walked the two blocks over to the Plaza. His portfolio contained three or four copies each of his current resume and list of references, copies he printed free at EDD.

Once he got to the job faire, he found there were a dozen or so employer tables rimming the outdoor plaza, each with at least one company recruiter. They always seemed a little smug to Neal, very self-confident. Sure, he thought, they already had secure jobs, so why not? At least fifty other people milled about the tables. Job hunters mostly. Some stood in line waiting to meet with prospective employers. Unfortunately, he did not see any food or refreshment tables. That sucked.

Neal headed over to the registration table, where an official-looking city employee greeted him and instructed him to find his name on the pre-referral list and sign off. A person had to be "invited" to this faire, which he had been through his EDD group. Only identified unemployed people were allowed to participate. Did Neal feel special? No, maybe a little like a loser. He searched the 'loser' list until he found his name, picked up a pen and signed in. He pocketed the pen—free gift.

"So, any refreshments served here today?" Neal asked the employee.

"Ah, you just missed them," she replied. "Ran out pretty quick today. I don't think they expected this many people to show up."

"Great," he mumbled.

"Well, you've got here a little late. The event's half over."

"Whatever."

Neal strolled away. Over the next hour or so, grumbling stomach and all, he made attempts to meet with employment representatives from five companies, just as he had been instructed to do by his employment development team leader. He had to report back to the group at their next meeting. He had mixed results, but overall he felt he did okay.

Banking: *So do you have any banking experience?* Well, not exactly, although I have had a bank account before with your institution. *Your resume says you've completed four years of college. What is your degree in?* Oh, well, it wasn't exactly four years, well maybe four years all combined. Neal did get to leave his resume with this company and the recruiter promised to keep it in file in case anything should come up in the future.

Life Insurance: *What exactly did you do most recently?* Sales, I was in Sales. *What did you enjoy about that?* Well, I really liked meeting new people, but I did not get along with my boss. *And why was that?* Well, I loved sales but I found it hard to work the hours that she expected. *What hours were those?* Well, like eight hours a day and I thought I could sell just as well in half that time! Neal was told his qualifications weren't quite right for the position they had available.

Computer Sales: *So you do have sales experience?* Yes, my last job. *And why did that job end?* Well, the company was cutting staff, downsizing, according to the letter I received. *How many employees were let go?* I'm not sure, I was asked not to return and I never heard anything from anyone else. *Did you receive severance pay, vacation pay, anything like that?* No, I didn't. *Well, you should have followed up with that.* I did, but they told me I hadn't worked there long enough. *How long was that?*

One month. That recruiter excused himself to "…make a phone call back to his office." Neal waited for ten minutes, hopeful that the recruiter was calling his office about him. But when the guy didn't come back after another ten minutes, Neal went to another table.

City Administration: *Says here on your resume you've had four years of college, State University?* Yes, I majored in English. *And so you received your BA?* Yes, but I lost my diploma when I moved recently. I'm sure I can get you a copy if you really need it. *Great and what type of position are you interested in?* Well, I can do most anything. I'm good with people, a hard worker. *Your last job was in sales?* Well, customer service really, not really sales. *In order to become a City employee, you will have to take a civil service exam.* You mean I'll be tested? *Yes and there will be an extensive background review if you pass that.* Oh, great, very good. Say, do you know if there are going to be any more refreshments served?

Neal decided he had enough.

Well, at least he could honestly report back to his EDD group next Thursday. Neal had completed his five interviews, although that counted the exchange with the person at the registration table as one of them. He took a seat for a minute on a concrete bench. These job fairs were grueling. Not having anything to eat or drink made it worse! Neal sighed. Screw it, he might finally have to bite the bullet and head over to the City-Search Ministry later. Someone had passed out a leaflet that stated free meals were served there on Thursday nights. Too bad they didn't start until six o'clock, he was already famished.

"Hey Neal!" It was Rachel.

She sat down next to him looking very sporty in a nice gray tweed business pants suit. Like him, she carried a portfolio file identical to the one Neal had gotten free from EDD on that first meeting.

"Hi, Rachel. You look nice. Any luck?"

She smiled a great big smile. "It was fun! And I don't really want to jinx it, but oh-my-god maybe I'll tell you later. A few of us are walking over to Harrison's. Happy hour starts in about a half hour. Come with us."

"Happy hour?" Neal hesitated.

"Come on, Neal. It'll be fun." She insisted. "They still serve great happy hour food, too."

His empty stomach reacted instinctively and growled.

"Oh, okay. That's Harrison's on 10th Street, right? I'll meet you there."

"Great! And don't bail on us this time!" She squeezed his hand, flashed him a smile and headed off.

§ § §

A few minutes later, Neal took a seat at a table for six in the fairly crowded bar. It was still a little early for the after-work crowd. Rachel and the others hadn't arrived yet. Perfect. A cocktail waitress approached.

"Can I get you something?" She was a cute brunette, a large red rose tattooed down one side of her neck.

"Hi, I'm waiting for some friends. Maybe just an ice water for now, with a lime, okay?"

"Yeah, be right back."

Neal watched her walk away, got up from the table and headed towards the bathrooms in back. A busboy was getting some warming trays ready for the free appetizers. The sight made him feel dizzy with delight and anticipation. Neal continued on and entered the men's room.

First he checked to make certain no one else was in there with him. Nope, empty. Neal walked over to the paper towel wall dispenser. Beneath it hung a metal trash receptacle. He lifted the plastic trash bag off the rim and reached his other hand beneath where extra replacement bags were sometimes stored. Yep, a bunch of them. Neal pulled one out, rolled it up and put it in his coat pocket, then exited.

When Neal got back to his table he found the waitress left him his water on a green napkin. He sat and took a sip.

Just then Rachel and two others he recognized from their EDD group came in. They saw Neal and came over to join him.

"Neal, you came!" Rachel gave him a quick little hug before taking a seat next to him.

The others said hello, shook hands and also took a seat.

"Okay," Rachel said excitedly. "I know I said I didn't want to jinx it, but I can't hold it in any longer. I think I got a job today!"

The excitement and congratulations around the table for her were warm and sincere. The small group had gotten to know each other a bit through their weekly meetings and job faire excursions. They had gotten to know the different circumstances that lead them all to the same predicament: unemployed and searching.

Except Neal. Neal kept his personal situation close to his vest. Unlike the others, he didn't feel the need to share and didn't want their sympathy in any way. But he was still happy for Rachel. And a little bit jealous, too.

"So what's the company?" he asked her. "And what do you mean 'you think'?"

"Well," she said to them. "I sat and interviewed with this guy, Jay Holstrup, from the McKinney Investment Group. They're hiring an admin assistant for one of their mortgage investment brokers and it looks like they want to hire me! Can you believe it? And the position could lead eventually to a mid-level investment position down the road. All I have to do is show up tomorrow at 8:00 a.m. and meet with the senior administrator, but it looks like I got it!"

"That's so great for you, Rachel."

"You were right, Neal. I just had to stay positive and look at what happened. Hey, first round is on me, guys! I'm buying!"

Amid the continued congrats and well wishes their waitress came over.

"Hi, this rounds on me," Rachel repeated. "And I'll have a vodka tonic, please."

"That sounds good to me, thanks Rachel," one of the others said.

"Me, too," replied the other.

Neal took a moment.

"You know," he said. "This special occasion calls for a special drink. I'm going to have a double shot of Knob Creek and a pint of stout."

"Yikes, Neal." Rachel was taken aback by Neal's order. "I haven't gotten the job yet, you know."

"Oh, I'm sorry," Neal replied. "I thought we were celebrating your good fortune. That's okay, I'll pay for that." And he made a grand gesture of reaching slowly inside his suit to the breast pocket, as if to pull out his wallet.

"No, no," Rachel said to the waitress. "I said I was buying this round and I meant it. No need to upset the good karma now. It's on me."

"Well, thanks, Rachel," Neal said. He pulled back his hand. He hadn't even brought his wallet in with him. It was sitting in his glove compartment. He smiled warmly. "And don't worry. I've got the next round."

As the conversation around the table continued Neal noticed the appetizers being brought out by a couple of waiters. About time.

He excused himself and went over by himself to check it out. Let's see, French fries, meatballs in barbeque sauce, and fried chicken wings. Yeah.

Neal picked up a small saucer from the stack and a fork. He grabbed a couple of napkins and stuffed them into his pants pocket. No one else came over. He was the first into the grub. Cool.

Soon Neal had French fries and chicken wings piled on his plate. With the plate being so small, he had to stack the food pretty high to get a fair amount to eat. No problem, he could come back as often as they kept refilling the trays.

Glancing back at his table, he saw his mates dealing with the waitress. Yum.

Neal quickly took his plate into the restroom and set it down carefully on the corner of the sink. Taking out the plastic bag, he emptied the fries and chicken into it and twisted the end closed. There was a little supply shelf in the back corner of the bathroom, with various plastic jugs full of hand soap, paper towels, toilet paper, etc. This would be a good stash to remember next time he needed some supplies. Neal placed his plastic bag of goodies behind one of the jugs and covered it up with a couple of paper towels, perfectly out of sight. Now it was time to refill his plate with appetizers again before heading back to the table to enjoy his drinks and grub.

By the time Neal finished his double shot and halfway through his beer chaser, he had gone back to the food table and added to his storage bag two more times. A good amount for dinner, maybe left-overs for breakfast even. And of course refilled his plate each time, too.

The others were just about finished with their first round of drinks, time for Neal to go. There would be no rounds on Neal. He was full of food and good drink and felt a nice pleasant warm buzz. The smile on his face showed he was happy and content.

To top things off, Neal had been able to scoop up seven dollars and some change from a couple of tables near the bathrooms. Tip money left for some waiter or waitress, which Neal gladly helped himself to. He truly believed when opportunity knocked, one had to answer.

Neal drained his glass with a low sigh and set the pint glass down. With a smile, he started, "Okay everybody —", but then stopped abruptly, reaching into his coat pocket. He smiled apologetically as he pulled out his cell phone, looked intently at the small call screen. "Oops — excuse me all, I've got to take this call."

And he left them, heading towards the back of the bar, silent phone pressed to his ear, a serious look on his face. It must have been something important.

Yeah, important all right.

Neal re-entered the bathroom and grabbed his self-made doggie bag. He tied the end up good and tight and stashed the bag inside his coat, under his left elbow. Neal exited the bathroom, keeping his cell phone up to his ear with his left hand and the bag out of sight. Returning to his table and friends, he did not retake his seat.

In half pantomime and half whisper so as not to disrupt his "important call", Neal explained, "I am so sorry, but I have to leave. A family emergency. No big deal, everyone's okay, but I have to deal with this. Sorry, I'll get the next round next time, promise. And Rachel, thanks for the cocktails and good time and congrats again!"

Neal bent to give her a quick hug, which Rachel returned. And as her friend left she caught the strong whiff of fried chicken.

Neal skipped out of Harrison's. What a great day it had turned out to be. Food, drinks, cash, and his friends none the wiser about him. If his luck kept up he'd probably get a job offer tomorrow, too, like Rachel. Just watch and see.

§ § §

Neal dropped his night's dinner in the front seat of his car and replaced his coat in the trunk. It wasn't very late at all, fairly early evening, but Neal was tired. It had been a good, long day. He decided to just take it easy the rest of the night. Take it easy and get ready for the grind again tomorrow. Hell, being homeless wasn't easy.

That night Neal stopped at a liquor store and used up five of his seven dollars to buy a pint of cheap vodka and the last two dollars for a porn magazine. He wanted to keep the party going for a while at least, wanted to keep the good karma, like Rachel had said. Once back in his car, he returned to his private gas station and parked in back, hopefully for an undisturbed night—out of view, out of sight.

GATEWAY

Based on the fable "The Miser and His Gold": A miser had a lump of gold that he buried in his yard, coming to look at the spot every day. One day he came to see it had been stolen, and he pulled out his hair as he loudly lamented. His neighbor told him to simply bury a stone in the same hole and stare at that each day, for surely that would have the same value as the unused gold once did.

The moral of the fable is: Wealth unused may as well not exist.

L ocal news reporter:
"This is Rebecca Weathers, reporting live for KHCT-TV. I'm here at Saunz Plaza, in the center of our city's downtown area. Early this morning an unidentified man was found unconscious behind the large pillar directly across from me. Local police arrived on the scene and the man was declared dead. Police have cordoned off the area to search for possible clues as to the cause of death. With the cold spell this city has been going through, authorities believe the man may have simply died from hypothermia, exposure to the elements. The deceased, who again has not been identified, was a homeless man that often frequented the Plaza area, according to witnesses interviewed."

The TV report cut to a man in green raingear, dark gloves, orange florescent vest and hat:

"He was just lying there when I started emptying the trashcans here. I tried to get him up. The body was frozen stiff, so cold out. The police don't really like them sleeping out here for too long. They usually move them along and not too nicely, either. He just didn't get up, no matter how loud I was. No matter what I tried. All the other times he was here, he woke up and took off. Not this morning though, no. He seemed like an okay guy, just nowhere else to go."

Next, the screen cut to a woman in a heavy hooded coat with matching scarf and gloves:

"I work in the Shakler Insurance Office right here in the Plaza. I've seen this homeless man pretty much every day since I started working here. What? Yeah, about six weeks. I get here around seven-thirty in the morning and he's always wrapped up on that bench there. Yeah, I guess right where they found him. It's very sad."

Then the news program cut to a man in a white chef's hat, green apron:

"My wife and I own this sandwich shop, yes, and we do open early in the mornings. Yes, coffee, teas, muffins, cakes, yes. Sometimes this guy would come in to ask for hot coffee, hot tea. You know sometimes we gave him something, not always. Once you start they kind of expect it always, you know? But when it gets so cold out there like lately we at least like to give some hot water, maybe coffee, yes. It's too bad that has to happen around here."

Next was a view of a man unloading boxes from the back of an SUV:

"Hey, you see these people pretty much everywhere. After a while it's hard to remember one from the other. But yeah, I think I remember seeing this guy around here sometimes. Hard to say, I travel all over the city and have a lot of stops. Like I said, they're pretty much all over."

§ § §

The Pearly Gates of Heaven:

"Okay, next. Yep, that's you. Come on, have a seat. Right here."

"What is this?"

"Just your entry interview. John Van Slyk, right, with a long 'I'? Did I pronounce that correctly? Middle name Anthony. That's a good name, John Anthony Van Slyk. I'm Peter, I'll be conducting your interview into Heaven."

"Yeah, that's me all right. So there really is a Pearly Gate?"

"Well, more like a modified titanium alloy overlaid with some sort of marble-granite-brass fusion. We get all the newfangled materials up here. Looks a bit like pearl though, you think? That's probably why everybody seems to think that."

"I'm in Heaven?"

"You, my good man, are just a few steps away. By the way, you're one of a very few number of newcomers who have ever asked me about those gates. I think most people are just glad to be here."

"Oh, I'm glad all right, don't get me wrong. Wait, Peter? Like St. Peter? At the Pearly Gates?"

"The living cliché himself, at your service! Well, not really at your service, but here to interview you for final entry. Come to think of it, not really 'living' either. At least not in the everyday sense. You ready?"

"This like a job interview?"

"Ha-ha, that's a good one, very funny, John. Job interview. I'll have to tell Mr. Hoffa that one, he'll get a kick out of that. No, not a job interview. I'm not sure why we even call it an interview. Consider it more like a little chat."

"A chat about what exactly? I was never one for chit-chat."

"Mmm, yes, we know. Just a conversation then, nothing more, nothing less. Just a final talk before you head on into Heaven."

"Anybody ever sent, you know, the other direction, based on this little conversation?"

"Actually, no, no one that I can think of off the top of my halo. Sorry, that's an Angel joke. But no, once you're here you're pretty much here for good reason. Of course, I haven't attended all of the entry chats, but I've handled quite a few over time, quite a few. Always interesting, I must say."

"Well, guess I'm ready if you are. Got nothing to lose, right?"

"Nothing to lose and all of Heaven's graces to gain, sir."

"Okay."

"Okay. So. What happened?"

"Huh, uh, excuse me? What do you mean what happened?"

"Well, what happened? To you?"

"Guess I screwed up all right. I mean, I'm dead, right?"

"In one sense, yes, you're right. No more earthly body. But in other ways you are more than ever alive and well."

"Well, okay, that's good, I guess. I feel good, anyway."

"So tell me, what happened?"

"Like I said, I screwed up. Pretty much been screwing up most of my life."

"So you blame yourself. For what?"

"Mmmm, lessee. Well, I lost my job a while back."

"Oh, yes, I can see from your file that you did. You were a night watchman?"

"Yeah, I lasted almost three months."

"What did you do to lose your job?"

"Guess I was late a few times. And for some reason it was hard for me to learn all the different combinations on all those door locks. They didn't want anyone to write them down, you know, in case someone got hold of the sheet."

"Well, says here you had some learning disability, that right?"

"Some doctor kept telling me and my folks that when I was a kid. Made all of the numbers and letters mix up."

"Right. Didn't your teachers, employers, your bosses, or maybe a doctor try to help you with that?"

"It never really came up. I've been dealing with it my whole life so I guess I just kinda forget about it. It was never much of a problem once I dropped out of school. I could always find odd jobs out there when I was young. They just never lasted very long. As I got older jobs were harder to come by until I couldn't find anything."

"Do you think maybe that's why you dropped out of school way back when? Classes must have been pretty tough when you couldn't read the words and didn't see the numbers correctly."

"I was always bored with school, it was never much fun. The kids would tease me because I was slow. Sometimes some of them just wouldn't let up but I was always good with my fists. That kept them quiet."

"The teachers should have tried to help you. There are ways to help with that problem, tutors, training and maybe even medication."

"We probably couldn't have afforded the help anyway. I just tried to take care of myself, didn't want to be a burden on anyone. And problems like that don't make a big difference when you're sleeping on a bench."

"Maybe they screwed up by not helping you. Helping is easy. You just have to want to do it. Well, just so you know you won't have that ailment anymore. And here you get all the help you need."

"That's sounds pretty good. What do I have to do?"

"There are plenty of resources and people who want to help. Just ask. Actually, it's simple because everyone wants to help and they just do."

"Anyway, like I said, I lost my job. Be kinda hard to pay."

"You know, no one in Heaven has a real 'job-job.' You're free to come and go about your business as you wish."

"Don't you have a job interviewing?"

"Oh, this isn't a job. I like to do this. In fact I volunteered once a long, long time ago. Liked it so much I just kept showing up to help. I always learn something new and interesting, as I said."

"Well, you can't just go about without a job in life. You need a job. I sure have been told that over and over a million times."

"Yes, I suppose that's what most everyone expects."

"Well, you need money. For a place to live. A house or an apartment or something. Your own place. Sounds simple but it sure ain't."

"Yep, that's something. But this is like a totally different life. You know, here no one owns their own home or anything."

"What do people do?"

"You'll be free to come and go about, just like everyone else. Stay where you want."

"What if it gets cold, or rains, what about at night?"

"Oh, the temperature's pretty neutral. Of course you can always go somewhere that's cooler or hotter or with snow. Whatever you like. And you should see the beautiful rainbows after it rains. Just gorgeous. And usually there's so much to do at night. So many people enjoy nights together."

"What about money for food?"

"Oh, there's food everywhere. And if you need something, just ask, someone will help show you how to get what you want, need or whatever. We all help each other here."

"Clothes?"

"Look, you're wearing some great clothes, aren't you? Clothes are no problem. They're everywhere, just use what you like. Some people love making them and sharing them with others, too. Like a hobby."

"Shoes, then. I haven't had a good pair of shoes for as long as I can remember."

"The latest urban street-wear to the most delicate satin slip-ons to the most rugged waterproof recreational gear. Even the latest in high tech synthetic foot gloves, the latest. I think some folks used to design shoes for Nike or Adidas or Sketchers and created these when they arrived. They're like walking on air. Which, by the way, you can do that, too, if you like."

"Walk on air? You mean fly?"

"Sort of. It's hard to describe, but you'll see when you get in. Actually, most people just go moving about in their bare feet. The ground actually feels like a constant foot massage. Just decide what you want and do it."

"And all of this stuff is free? I just have to want it, pick it up, or think it?"

"NOW you're getting it! But of course the concept of being 'free' doesn't really pertain to Heaven. It's sort of like your thoughts become your reality. Well, wait now, now that I think about it, maybe that 'free' concept is what Heaven is all about. Hmm, something to discuss later at HQ."

"Heaven has a headquarters?"

"Oh no! HQ is Holy Quest. Although, again, you could have an HQ/headquarters if you want one, anyone could."

"What's Holy Quest?"

"Well, that's just a bunch of us getting together, sitting around and discussing greater thoughts and infinite topics. Enjoying each other's company. So many interesting people and stories."

"Where do you do this?"

"Anywhere we want, really. Anytime."

"Kind of sounds like hanging out. Folks didn't like it when me and my friends would just hang out somewhere. Even if a place was made for hanging out, like in the park or at a bus stop or on a bench."

"Why not?"

"Not sure. It was pretty much the same thing you described, talk about everything and anything, and enjoy each other's company. But folks catch me and my friends doing that, boy would they get upset. Called the cops most of the time if we didn't move out when they wanted us to."

"Were you bothering them?"

"Not that I know of. I think they were scared of us."

"Did you try to scare them?"

"Naw, I think they just didn't know us. Kids are taught not to mess with strangers so strangers must be scary to people even when they get older. I guess I should have taken the time to talk to people more, explain things more. Not sure they wanted to listen to me though."

"There you go, taking the blame again. Maybe they should have just let you hang out. Doesn't seem like you were bothering anybody. Seems like you were on an HQ."

"Rules, I guess. I probably wasn't following the rules. Lots of rules out there."

"Somebody's rules, but not the rules here. Must have been hard for folks to see the possibility of a Holy Quest going on. But you can hang out with me anytime you want, once you get in. When you're ready."

"Well, okay."

"Okay, then."

"Anything else?"

"Anything else what?"

"Anything else to talk about, before, you know, before I get into Heaven."

"Do you have anything?"

"I don't think so, no, not really. I do want to apologize for messing things up, not taking care of myself and all."

"Look, it seems pretty clear from talking to you that maybe a lot of your issues could have been taken care of. Sometimes people just need a little help. So, now answer my question: What happened?"

"I should have gotten more help, should have asked for more help."

"And you should have been given all of the help you needed. That's all. Simple, really. And that's what this place is: simple. What you need, you get, because everyone is willing to help you. Once you don't really need anything else, you'll find yourself helping others. Helping is simple and contagious."

"Wow! Sounds like—"

"Heaven? Yes, it does, doesn't it? Head on in."

§ § §

Local news reporter:

"If identified, the man's family will be notified. If no help is received, the County Coroner's Office will handle the remains. Please call the City Police Desk at 555-9977, ext. 2425, if you think you can help identify the deceased or have any information about this death. Later in this broadcast, our own KHCT anchorman, Jerry Morse, will have an exclusive interview with Police Chief Erwin Morse about the growing homelessness problem in our town. This is Rebecca Weathers, reporting live for KHCT-TV, local news. Back to you in the studio, Jerry."

FRAYED ENDS

A disjointed woman's voice floated briefly above the low noise. The respectful harmonious discord had grown over the last few minutes with the arrival of more visitors.

"Thank you all so much for coming. We're going to get started with the program in just a few minutes."

A few handkerchiefs and paper napkins fluttered, wiping warm brows. Even more had unashamed tears. Guests were filling the rows of metal folding chairs lined up into two uneven sections in the room. One section had eight chairs per row, the other only six. A four-foot aisle remained clear between the sections. All of the chairs faced a make-shift stage and wooden podium situated at one end of the room. A small shrine of cut flowers in vases of various colors, sizes, and shapes had been created on a small four-legged folding table on the raised stage. The table was covered in a brown, lacy tablecloth.

A single bright-white sheet of heavy stock had been folded in two to make a card and was propped up in front of the vases. The card stood out starkly against the array of colorful flowers. Even from a distance, one could make out the words on the card, handwritten in nice cursive penmanship with blue and black markers: Rest in Peace, Our Brother. One could imagine the card's creator trying so hard to write neatly and in a straight line, unable to overcome a noticeable slant to the words.

In between the podium and the table of flowers, an enlarged picture rested on a small aluminum easel. A photo of a smiling man, bushy beard and eyebrows, dark eyes stared directly into the camera. If you looked directly at the picture you felt the man was watching you, but not in an uncomfortable way.

Voices and snatches of conversation murmured throughout the crowded waiting room, words fading in and out of hearing range.

121

"Unbelievable one person could touch so many people. He helped so many of our brothers."

"There are some more chairs up here, if you want to take a seat."

"He was a fine man, a fine man."

Lydia was holding Rose's hand, a habit when there were other people around. The gesture was as much for her comfort as Rose's.

"Come on, Rose, let's sit up there in the front." She led her daughter to some empty seats. Rose focused on the blue paper program she held while Lydia gazed at the man's photo.

"Tragic. He really turned his life around."

"I only spoke to him once, but he really did everything he could to try to help me."

"So sad. Such a shock to everyone."

Neal stood in the crowd at the rear of the room, leaning his back up against the wall farthest from the stage and podium.

"What the hell is this crap?" he thought to himself.

Great, he didn't come here for this. Irritated and trying to make himself even more invisible, he nervously rubbed at a couple of spots he just noticed on the front of his jacket. More and more dirty spots were showing up on his clothes and nothing exasperated him more.

"More seats up front!"

"Program? Would you like one?"

"Did he have any family, do you know?"

Sascha sat off to one side, alone in her thoughts, empty seats on either side of her. These services were getting to be old hat to her. They seemed to happen every other week or so now. She looked at the display set up on the makeshift stage, thrown together by friends, coworkers, family? Obviously, Sascha wasn't the only one who didn't know if the guy even had family.

"So many bad people out there and it happened to this wonderful man."

"I didn't really know him that well, but so many people told me about him."

"If you didn't know him, he would have scared you. But he was the kindest man I ever met."

Marilyn sat in the front of the room, waiting for everyone to gather and settle. Hopefully, the nervous energy of the room would calm before the program started. She stared at the front wall for a time, then at the flowers she, and others, had brought. Finally Marilyn allowed herself to look at his photo and felt her heart shudder again. Her sadness was overwhelming, but knew she needed to do this, knew having this ceremony was at least one way to honor a good person with a good heart—a kindred spirit. Marilyn stared at the picture and thought, "The world is going to miss you so much."

Suddenly, she thought about her husband, Dan, and her daughter, Janie. They were sad about the whole thing, especially Dan. Thank God Scotty was too young. If only she could have done more to comfort Dan and Janie, but it was so hard with her grieving as well. This morning Marilyn had sworn to make it up to them by cutting back her time at work, just as soon as the State budgets were approved and signed off. She would.

Finally, the grieving Marilyn turned so she was partially facing the still gathering crowd. Some of the faces were familiar. Some were only brief acquaintances, others more so, but she did not acknowledge any of them. Marilyn didn't even look to acknowledge her husband and daughter, who were there somewhere. Her body and mind just felt tired, empty.

"Truly sad, what happened. I wish I had known him better."

"How did it happen? He was so strong and was doing so much."

"You never know, really, one slip up is all it takes. All that heartache."

Lydia took a long look at the face of the man in the picture. The picture showed him with a smile, but if you looked carefully she thought she could see pain behind that smile. And his eyes were strong, tough and wary, she thought. She draped an arm around Rose and squeezed her tightly.

"Rose, you'll take care of me, right?" She gave her daughter another quick hug. As she squeezed Rose, Lydia's breath caught momentarily.

"You know I will, mama," Rose replied, patting her mother on the back. "We will always take care of each other."

"It's not always going to be like this, Rose. We'll work it out, get back on our feet and get settled."

"Just a little time, mama. I know. It's just going to take a little time." She kissed her mama on the cheek and settled back in her chair. But Rose also thought, "We've got lots and lots of time, now we just need a little help. Or a lot of luck."

Neal tapped the shoulder of a man handing out programs, one-page sheets of light blue paper, quickly created for the occasion. A small picture of the deceased was on the front, folded over with printed writing on the inside flap. It was the same picture as the one in front of the room. Neal scanned over the verse printed on one side of the inside fold:

"The strife is o'er, the battle done. Now is the Victor's triumph won.
O let the song of praise be sung, alleluia!
Death's might pow'rs have done their worst But Jesus has his foes dispersed.
Let shouts of praise and joy outburst, alleluia!
He closed the yawning gates of hell. The bars from heav'n's high portals fell.
Let hymns of praise his triumph tell, alleluia!"
(from "The Strife Is O'er", tr. Francis Pott, 1859).

Neal sighed, feeling more impatient, and grabbed the gentleman handing out the programs on the sleeve of his coat. The man was startled for a moment and dropped one of the programs, which floated lazily to the floor. The man turned to Neal sharply.

"Excuse me," Neal said. Quickly reaching down, Neal swooped up the program and handed it back to the gentleman in one motion. "I'm not sure what's going on today, but do you know the person I see about staying here tonight? I called ECHO Shelter Services and they said they would send a referral over here." He read to him from a little piece of paper. "Is there a Marilyn Hampton available?"

"We're having a memorial service for a dear friend and volunteer, as you can see," the gentleman replied. "Marilyn will be available afterwards, I think. You're welcome to stay and wait."

124

"Do you know if there are any available spots? I really need a place to stay tonight. If I wait too long, I may miss out on a space at some other shelter."

"I'm not sure, but Marilyn would know. Or you might want to check with one of the other advocates after the service. They'll be able to help you, too." The man stepped away.

Neal rolled his eyes and sighed. Great, now he had to sit through this sad service for someone he didn't even know! And he was exhausted. Neal hadn't slept a minute in that damned holding cell. At least he was out of that hellhole. And maybe they would be serving food or refreshments after this thing, if he was lucky. Still, he was going to have to figure a way to get his car currently locked in the City's impound lot. Just great.

Whatever, just more crap to deal with. Neal shrugged his shoulders. There was one empty seat along the crowded back row and Neal sat down. He carried a brown paper grocery bag that held his toiletry case, towel, and change of underclothes. There was enough room under his chair and Neal shoved his bag there, settling in his seat. He muttered under his breath, "Freaking-A great."

"You know he got me that job working at that AM/PM gas station on 13th Avenue. If not for that I don't know where I'd be."

"Remember that first night we came here to City Search and he cussed you out, man? Dude was gonna kick your butt."

"Yeah, that's right. But you and I both know that was just what I needed. Dude was tough, tough but right on."

Sascha thought she recognized a person sitting a couple of rows in front of her—someone from one of her nights in the police cell. Why would that bitch be here? Sascha figured that whore would be doing some real time by now, mean and crazy as she was. Bitch better not be staying here at the shelter tonight, or there was going to be some trouble for sure.

"Whatever happened to that woman that talked all the time? The one with all of the bags of cleaning stuff?"

"Yeah, that Mrs. K-something. We haven't seen her around here for a while."

"I hope she's all right. I know this man took good care of her, tried to get her set up, you know."

(Unbeknownst to all at the shelter ceremony and lost in her own thoughts, Mrs. Kreiberg had found another comforting place near her husband's gravesite, where she could just sit and wait and watch the clouds and the world spin past her.)

Marilyn took a deep breath, rose from her seat and walked over to stand at the podium. There was no microphone, as the room was not that large.

"Ladies and gentlemen, friends, all of you, thank you so much for coming." She stood patiently, quietly, until the final murmurs died down. "First, I'd like to introduce Pastor Richard. I'm sure most of you know him well. Pastor?"

A frail-looking, mocha-skinned man shuffled slowly to the podium. He wore a white pastor's collar beneath his black shirt. The man had on faded blue jeans and dark hiking boots and carried a small leather-bound Bible that had to be at least a couple of generations old with use. He gave Marilyn a long, strong hug. Everyone knew Pastor Richard's frail look belied his great energy and strength, both internal and external. It was hard for anyone to keep up with him at the Ministry office. The hug broke and the Pastor stepped to the podium.

"Thank you, Marilyn. And thank you all for joining us today at this sad and, at the same time, joyful occasion. Before we start with our memorial service honoring a great, great man and our beloved friend and co-worker..."

He had to stop for a moment to take a deep breath.

"Okay," Pastor Richard continued. "May we please take a moment of silence to remember two others of our family who have recently passed? Please bow your heads at the sad losses and in memory of our dear, departed friends, John Van Slyk and Big Maceo Cleveland. May they be forever blessed as they are welcomed into the Kingdom of Our Lord's Heaven, warm and full with the grace of God's love."

Silence filled the room. A low sniffle or two, a chair scraping, hushed breathing. Hushed in tribute to the fallen.

"Thank you. Please bow your heads and let us pray:

My brothers and sisters, we come together today to remember our friends who have gone before us. We believe that the bonds uniting us in life do not dissolve with death, whether those bonds are bonds of struggle or bonds of bounty, bonds of sadness or bonds of joy, bonds of need or bonds of compassion. We know the choices we make now, in this time, lead us on our eternal path. And may the Good Lord help us keep to the straight and true path, the tried and true path, the one path to Love. Let us help those who stray along that journey, who may make choices that lead them astray, who find themselves in hopeless circumstances beyond their ability to manage. Let us heed the word of the Lord, who challenges us to love one another, to offer friendship and consolation to those we meet, for what we do unto others we surely do unto Him."

Then Pastor Richard raised his right palm in solemn blessing to the people gathered there:

"To our beloved friend and brother, Travis Waller, and to all who gather here to pay tribute: Friend, may you be free from suffering, be free from the longing for love, be free from hopelessness. Brother Travis, may you enjoy abundance, love, a warm heart, and a warm home. Amen, alleluia."

And, with a final nod to the crowd, Pastor Richard resumed his seat in the front row. Marilyn returned to the podium to continue the memorial program.

"Thank you, Pastor Richard. And thank you all again for coming today." She took a moment to solemnly look over the gathering and continued.

"As Pastor Richard prayed, there is a path for us on this Earth to travel. The choices we make start the ripples of our journey. We don't always know how those ripples will expand or how our own life choices create a greater impact down the road. Travis Waller made many choices during his life, some good, some bad. Like all of us, he struggled to handle the demands of his time. Yet, even as he struggled personally, Travis Waller found strength through giving to others, in helping those who needed help."

Marilyn had to stop to dab at the tears welling in her eyes. She had to stop, breathe, breathe. Marilyn shook her head and looked around the room. One deeper sigh before she could continue.

"I'm not sure, but I wonder if I could have done more to help him. To understand the demons and issues he was trying to deal with. He always tried so hard for others and gave so little attention to himself, to his own needs. Could I have tried harder?"

And now the tears flowed freely and Marilyn sobbed behind her handkerchief. Amid attempted consoling comments from the crowd ("It was his time." "You did your best." "Not your fault, Marilyn."), Pastor Richard stepped up to her, wrapped one arm around her shoulders and patted her there to comfort her. She went on as best she could in halted voice.

"We have lost a great man, as you all came to know him in his short time here with us. He tried so hard, but in the end made a couple of bad choices. Now we have lost him. One of the first things I told Travis Waller was that we would do the best we could but we couldn't help every person every night. From the moment I told him that, he tried to prove me wrong. He made it his goal to help everybody, every day and every night."

Marilyn had to stop. She couldn't go on, didn't know what more to say. She looked at the picture of Travis Waller, then stepped closer to briefly, gently touch the face of the man in the photo. She sadly smiled to the people in attendance and resumed her seat.

Pastor Richard replaced Marilyn at the podium.

"Let's just give Miss Marilyn a minute or two before we resume the program, okay? I know this is hard on all of us. Would anyone like to say a few words in honor of our beloved brother, Travis?"

There were a few moments of the usual nervous silence as people questioned their own strength and resolve in paying their respects to a fallen friend, out loud, to others.

"Rose," Lydia whispered. "We should say something. Come on, you and me. Travis was a good person, he wanted to help us."

"I don't know what to say, mama. You go ahead, if you want." Neither of them did.

Sascha burrowed herself deeper into the hood of her coat. "Hey,

I barely knew the guy," she thought. "He seemed nice and all, but I don't think anyone wants to hear what I have to say."

Neal was indignant in his seat, bristling at the thought of further delay. "Crap, I got plenty to say," he muttered to himself. He seethed inside. "What the hell. When's the food being served? Can I get a room or should I just sleep out on some park bench like the rest of you losers?"

Marilyn was tired and so sad. She felt deflated.

Pastor Richard replied, "It's okay if you'd rather not. We'll also make some time later for those of you who would like to pay your respects, share your words, memories, or stories."

Just then a man and a young girl rose up from their seats on one side of the room. The man said, "I have a few words to share."

The gentleman embraced the Pastor as they gained the podium. Then Pastor Richard knelt to hug the man's daughter. As the Pastor rose the man spoke to the gathering.

"Hi, everyone. I hope I can do this, this is really hard."

The young girl at his side moved in closer and he draped an arm caringly about her shoulders. She was very pretty with long dark hair and a sad smile as she looked up at him. Tears were already falling down her ruddy pink cheeks.

"I'm Dan. I'm married to Marilyn. And this is our daughter, Jane." He stopped to take a deep shuddering breath to pull himself together.

"It's okay, Daddy," the girl said to her father. "You can tell them about Mr. Waller—Travis. It's important."

His daughter's words seemed to give him strength. Dan nodded. He saw Marilyn smile at them through her tears and that helped, too.

"Okay, I will, Jane. Thanks, everybody. Thanks for bearing with me. We would like to tell you a story. A story about Travis Waller."

And he squeezed the young girl's shoulders again, smiled down at her. He resumed.

"But the story's really about me and my daughter. You see, I knew Travis Waller many, many years ago. Jane met him last year. And he was our hero."

Acknowledgements

Thank you to Ken Tupper, Owner/Publisher of Divertir Publishing, for skill, creativity and giving me the opportunity to share my stories; Divertir staff supreme, Jayde Gilmore, Senior Editor, and Jen Corkill Hunt, Acquisitions Editor, for working with me to improve this collection and for teaching me so many new things; and, to the Divertir Publishing staff for your generosity and willingness to support the Midway Shelter, Alameda.

Eternal gratitude and much love to my wife, Sue, who read, reread, and edited so many story iterations and gave me the final brilliant recommendation to tie these stories together. Because of that we were able to reveal how homelessness creates its own subtle subcultures in seemingly disparate and non-connected environments.

To my many friends, family members and co-workers, with whom I shared many of these stories and received invaluable feedback in return. You have all added a piece of yourself to these final fables and for this I am so appreciative.

To all the selfless people who work directly to help the homeless, on the street, in clinics, in shelters, churches, food banks, and everywhere on the front lines, you are all heroes. And to those countless folks, like me, who work behind the scenes in support of the effort, on budgets and reports, on databases and paper, on laws and policies, creating and maintaining the infrastructure to continue service, you are vital and important. Homelessness was supposed to be a short-term problem, but we have all learned otherwise, and we keep our shoulders to the grindstone, fighting the good fight, supporting each other along the way. I am proud to count myself as a friend among you.

Dear readers,

I hope you enjoy this book. I am indebted to you all for allowing my perspectives and perceptions into your life and for letting me share my simple message about homeless people: they are us.

About the Author

 In his spare time, Phil Canalin works in public health finance, most recently for the noted Alameda County Health Care for the Homeless Program. He also loves to write fiction, short stories, poetry, and children's stories. This is his first published short story collection based on his rare opportunities to observe, work with, and speak to homeless people and the dedicated people that serve and care for them. Phil's first published novel is titled *Slow Pitch Softball – More Than Just A Game* (Black Rose Writing, 2013). He also has a published children's book, *Just Hug A Bubble!*, and collaborated on a cookbook project with his wife, Sue, *Dinner at the Sonneman's*. Phil resides in Alameda, CA with Sue, his high-school sweetheart and wife of 34 years. Daughters, Jessica and Kelsey, live in Hawaii and NorCal, respectively, both enviably facing the beach. Phil grew up loving Aesop's Fables and The Rocky and Bullwinkle Show's Fractured Fairy Tales and Aesop & Son.

Check out Phil, his blog and other writing projects at
http://www.philcanalin.com
and look for his next publication!

133

Also by Divertir Publishing

Right there, on the gray cinderblock wall, was a
jet-black piece of graffiti that I couldn't quite
understand at first. Miriam must have caught
the look on my face because she explained. "It's
a map of Haiti," she said. It made sense
suddenly. The map of Haiti had an eye placed
in it so that it looked like a face. Coming down
from the eye was a single giant tear drop.
"Haiti is weeping."

On Tuesday, January 12th 2010, a magnitude 7.0 earthquake
shook the island nation of Haiti. The United States Agency for
International Development estimated the death toll to be somewhere
between 46,000 and 85,000 people, with 220,000 injured and over 1.5
million homeless. Many organizations, both from the U.S. and
abroad, responded to the appeal for humanitarian aid.

Dr. Stephen Schroering and Chris Rakunas went to Haiti to
deliver over 21,000 pounds of medical and surgical supplies to the
New Life Children's Home in Port-au-Prince, Haiti, and several
other hospitals. In Tears for the Mountain, Chris recounts his
mission to deliver these supplies to the earthquake-ravaged island
nation. Chris discusses both the triumphs and heartbreaks of the
trip, the problems with distributing aid in a nation lacking the most
basic infrastructure, and his unexpected encounter with a notorious
Haitian warlord.

*A portion of the proceeds for this book will be donated to the New Life
Children's Home in Port-au-Prince, Haiti.*

Made in United States
North Haven, CT
26 November 2022

27315399R00078